12 Million Black Voices

S0-BBR-408

12 Million Black Voices

Text by
RICHARD WRIGHT

Photo direction by
EDWIN ROSSKAM

LIBRARY
COLBY-SAWYER COLLEG
NEW LONDON, NH 03257

THUNDER'S MOUTH PRESS

NEW YORK

E 185.6 W9 1988
OCLC 16868125
12 million black voices /
Wright, Richard.

Copyright © 1941 Richard Wright—text and captions

Photographic rights are credited in

the list of acknowledgements, page 149

Foreword copyright © 1988 by David Bradley

Published in the United States by

THUNDER'S MOUTH PRESS

841 Broadway, Fourth Floor

New York, NY 10003

Cover design by Brack Bivins

Grateful acknowledgement is made to the New York State Council

on the Arts and the National Endowment for the Arts for

financial assistance with the publication of this work.

Library of Congress Cataloging-in-Publication Data

12 million black voices / text by Richard Wright :

photo direction by Edwin Rosskam.   p.   cm.

    Previously published: 12 million black voices : a folk history of the Negro in the
United States. New York : Viking Press, 1941.

    Chiefly photographs collected by the Farm Security Administration.

    ISBN 0-938410-44-X

    1. Afro-Americans—Social conditions—To 1964. 2. Afro-Americans—Social condi-
tions—To 1964—Pictoral works. I. Wright, Richard,

1908-1960.   II. Rosskam, Edwin,1903–   . III United States. Farm

Security Administration.   IV. Title.   V. Title: 12 million black voices.

E185.86.A13   1988

973'.0496073—dc19   87-26454   CIP

This edition ISBN 1–56025–247–2

Manufactured in the United States of America

Distributed in the U.S.A. by:

Publishers Group West

1700 Fourth Street

Berkeley, CA 94710

Preface

NINETEEN FIFTEEN. Henry Ford produced his first farm tractor. Jack "Li'l Arthur" Johnson, the once-defiant black heavyweight, took a dive in Cuba, yielding the championship to Jess Willard, the latest Great White Hope. D. W. Griffith's The Clansman, retitled Birth of a Nation, was released with the enthusiastic support of President Woodrow Wilson and the enthusiastic opposition of the National Association for the Advancement of Colored People and its director of publications, W. E. B. Du Bois. The resurgent Ku Klux Klan met on Stone Mountain in Georgia for its first-ever cross burning. Fifty-six blacks were reported lynched. And the Great Migration began to change the complexion of America.

At the beginning of the twentieth century, the face of America was a study in contrast. The North was white, a nation of white natives and immigrants. The South was—mottled. Ninety percent of America's blacks lived there; in some areas, the precincts of the so-called Black Belt, they outnumbered whites. As American industry was still heavily concentrated in the North in 1910, more than half of the employed black population worked in agriculture, the overwhelming majority as Southern "sharecroppers," with a legal and social status little different from that enjoyed by their slave grandfathers. Less than 13 percent of the black work force was involved in manufacturing and industry. By contrast, a congressional commission reported that, in the twenty-one industries it surveyed, nearly 58 percent of the workers were immigrants, most from southern and eastern Europe.

But by 1920, the number of black farm workers had decreased by nearly half, while the number of black industrial laborers had increased by a third. For during the intervening decade a stream of blacks had flowed from Southern counties to Northern cities. About 1915, the stream swelled to a river—between 1915 and 1918, 500,000 black men braved the discouragement of Southern landowners and the Ku Klux Klan (which, essentially, exhorted ''good'' Negroes to stay home to be lynching fodder) and made the journey north. In the classic immigrant pattern, they found whatever work they could, saved, and sent for their kin—first brothers, cousins, uncles, who found more work and sent money home, then mothers, wives, children.

Water flows because of gravity. People flow because of symbols and hope. European immigrants became a cross-current in the Atlantic Ocean because the Statue of Liberty, in the words of Emma Lazarus, invited the tired, the poor, huddled masses to enter America's Golden Door. (Never mind that Lazarus was in Europe when she wrote ''The New Colossus,'' and died before she could see the Statue of Liberty, let alone the immigrant hordes.) Black migrants became a river across the land because their slave forebears had dreamed that the North Star pointed the way to a mythic ''Freedom Land'' where blacks were free and unpersecuted. In slave days, Northern realities were unreported and very much beside the point. What black would complain about the North's ''gradual emancipation'' when in the South any emancipation was illegal? Who would carp about the North's second-class citizenship when in the South blacks had the legal status of a mule? During the Civil War even these realities were swept beneath a rug of propaganda; the North was portrayed as the Land of Lincoln the Liberator—the birthplace of Yankees who died to make men free.

The myth survived war and Reconstruction. For although Southern freedom failed in 1877, when, in a room in Wormley's Hotel, presidential candidates Rutherford B. Hayes and Samuel J. Tilden became strange bedfellows to resolve the disputed election (Hayes became president, while the control of

Southern politics was restored to the ex-Confederates), few blacks knew the details of the coupling; from their point of view, it only seemed that Jim Crow had been immaculately conceived and antiblack terrorism spontaneously generated, when Hayes, as part of the compromise, withdrew federal troops from the South. And so, on into the next century, the North retained a mythic quality in the hearts and minds of Southern sharecroppers. And in 1915, as the Klan killed blacks and repeatedly replayed the new ritual of cross burning, and as it became ever more clear that sharecropping was de facto slavery (as Du Bois reported: " 'What rent do you pay here,' I inquired. . . . 'All we make,' answered Sam.''), black migrants hopped northbound freights for the same reason white immigrants had boarded westbound freighters. As Emma Lazarus might have put it, they were tired, and poor, and yearned to breathe free.

And so the face of the American North darkened as black migrants flowed into the cities. There, as had white immigrants and earlier black migrants, they settled together in urban villages, held together by kinship, place of origin, and shared religion and custom. They adapted those customs to the Northern reality and developed new customs. Like a river forming a delta, they added rich and fertile cultural soil to the North—the ''Renaissance'' they brought to Harlem was duplicated in many ways in a dozen cities. In Chicago, in 1915, their numbers supported the founding of the North's first black insurance company and of the Association for the Study of Negro Life and History. Two years later, Joe ''King'' Oliver, brought New Orleans jazz ''up the river'' from Storyville to Chicago, and in the next decade his Creole Jazz Band would be the training ground for a generation of black musicians, including Louis Armstrong.

Water does not respond to that which is absolute, but rather to that which is relative. The realities of America (Ellis Island, the quota system, discrimination—No Irish Need Apply) may have discouraged some immigrants, but relatively speaking, they were better off, and so sang the praises of America the Free. So it was with the migrants. The jobs they found were low-paying, menial and exhausting by Northern industrial standards, but lucrative, high-status and relatively easy by Southern agricultural ones—ten hours sweeping a factory were nothing compared to twelve hours behind a mule. The oppressions they found were relatively mild—who would complain about police brutality and biased justice when in the South any group of white men could be cop, judge, jury and executioner? Who would carp about a stinking toilet down the hall when in the South the toilet was in the yard, and smelled worse? Few bad reports returned to the South, and so the river flowed, and pooled in sections of Northern cities the immigrants abandoned. It was better there. It truly was.

But the absolute, as opposed to relative, truth was that Northern racism was every bit as virulent as the Southern strain. Above the Mason-Dixon line black people did not so often swing from trees (although lynching had its moments), but principles of mass production were invoked. In 1917, although thirty-six blacks were reported lynched (and most lynchings were of course unreported), there were two union-instigated race riots in East St. Louis, Illinois, and a congressional investigating committee reported, "It is not possible to give accurately the number of dead. At least thirty-nine Negroes and eight white people were killed outright, and hundreds of Negroes were wounded and maimed. 'The bodies of the dead Negroes,' testified an eye witness, 'were thrown into a morgue like so many hogs.'" Ten thousand blacks marched down Fifth Avenue in a silent parade protesting the nationwide violence. In 1918, while sixty blacks were reported lynched, there were riots in Philadelphia and in nearby Chester, Pennsylvania. In 1919, while seventy-six blacks were reported lynched, six people were killed and a hundred wounded, in a riot in the nation's capital, and troops were mobilized to put down a Chicago riot in which fifteen whites and twenty-three blacks were killed, and more than five hundred people of both races were injured. And in addition to such blatant manifestations, Northern racism, like the Southern strain, had its subtle symptoms. Black people were crucified en masse on a Cross of Gold—segregated into high-priced run-down ghettos by landlords, preyed upon by cynical businessmen, black as well as white.

Still the migrants flowed North, full of hope. Between 1920 and 1930, 1.3 million blacks flowed out of the South–half a million in 1923 alone. The river pooled in the Northern cities; in New York, 92,000 blacks in 1910 became 327,000 by 1930. In Chicago, 44,000 became 233,000. In Detroit, 6,000 became, almost unbelievably, 120,000. Their hope was that the vast prosperity of the nation would trickle down, that unionization in industry would change things. Prosperity failed them; indeed, their swelling numbers, demanding housing, any kind of housing, made for a white-owned real estate boom. The Labor Movement failed them; in 1931, twenty-four unions, ten of them American Federation of Labor (AFL) affiliates, barred blacks entirely, and others discriminated in other ways. Blacks who migrated to Detroit to build cars found that the United Auto Workers maintained separate seniority lists for blacks and whites and supported a policy of keeping blacks out of skilled positions. Blacks who sought to work even in the lowest levels of the burgeoning film industry found that the Motion Picture Projectionists Union would not allow them to change reels anywhere in New York but Harlem. Nor was the failure of labor explained entirely by a fear of competition; blacks who organized in jobs that were *already* black found themselves unwelcome—the AFL twice refused to charter the Brotherhood of Sleeping Car Porters, and eventually did so only after the AFL was threatened by the secession of the Committee for Industrial Organization (CIO). But where hope failed there was irony.

Nineteen twenty-nine. Herbert Hoover, installed as the thirty-first president, proclaimed that "We in America today are nearer to the final triumph over poverty than ever before in the history of any land. The poorhouse is vanishing from us." It seemed a reasonable statement. Prosperity was everywhere. The stock market was reaching new highs week by week. The United States accounted for over a third of worldwide industrial production. Construction began on the Empire State Building. The stock market climbed like an arrow shot into the air. But on October 24, "Black Thursday," the market fell to earth. Nearly 13 million shares were sold on that day. Five days later sales rose to 16.4 million shares. By 1933, stocks valued at $87 billion were selling—if there were buyers—for $19 billion. Real-estate fortunes vanished—there was no profit in exorbitant rents that none could afford to pay.

But hardship too is relative. Although the Depression hurt blacks badly—eventually, 26 percent of black males and 32 percent of black females would be out of work and one in four blacks would be on relief—it hurt everyone badly. By 1933, between 15 and 17 million people were unemployed, industrial production had fallen by half, over 5,700 banks had failed, and the value of agricultural products had fallen from $8.5 billion to $4 billion. Although blacks lost much, the simple, sad fact was they had less to lose. They were already being paid 30 percent less than whites on the average, and were already crowded in substandard living conditions little better than the Hooverville shack cities that sprouted across the land. As prosperity fled, some whites began to see the black masses as a source of votes and power. The Communist party moved swiftly to court them. So did the Democratic party. The Labor Movement fractured and the newly organized Congress of Industrial Organizations,* which sought to organize the workers by industry instead of by craft, as had the old AFL, enrolled unskilled workers, many of whom were black. And relief, too, was relative.

Nineteen thirty-three. Adolf Hitler became chancellor of Germany—sixty thousand artists, musicians, actors and authors emigrated to the United States. Japan withdrew from the League of Nations. Franklin D. Roosevelt, elected with the help of two million Northern blacks, was inaugurated the thirty-second president of the United States and was granted by a desperate Congress broad (some would say dictatorial, the Supreme Court eventually would say unconstitutional) powers to deal with the chaos of the Great Depression. The Roosevelt administration established numerous agencies to deliver relief to the American public. Theoretically, the relief was granted equally. In fact, it was created in the racist image of American society. Under the National Industrial

*In 1938, the name of the "Committee for Industrial Organization" was changed to the "Congress of Industrial Organizations."

Recovery Act, for example, cost-of-living standards were established which discriminated against groups in which blacks were most likely to be found, and in such industries as steel, laundry and tobacco, black workers received lower minimum wages than whites. Under the Agricultural Adjustment Administration (AAA), the benefits of farm relief went primarily to landowners rather than to the tenants who actually worked the land. Under the Social Security Board, unemployment benefits were provided to workers—but domestic and agricultural workers (who were mostly black) were exempted, and even under the provisions granting old-age pensions, whites usually received larger grants than blacks. But some money trickled through. In the National Youth Administration, a full 10 percent of the student-work-program enrollees were black. The Home Owners' Loan Corporation made it possible for some blacks to purchase houses, thereby escaping the cycle of landlord-tenant oppression that had pursued them from Black Belt to ghetto. The Federal Housing Administration gave some blacks the ability to build houses of their own. Although many of the New Deal programs supported segregation, with whatever negative psychological consequences that may have had, material benefits were often positive. The segregated Civilian Conservation Corps put 200,000 black teenagers to work, and gave them a basic eduation and black supervisors as role models. The Work Projects Administration (WPA), although it never employed as many blacks as it was supposed to, nevertheless constructed black hospitals, college buildings and playgrounds.

And the Roosevelt administration, although hardly perfect in this regard, sent the message to the country that blacks were to be consulted, at least in areas which concerned their welfare. Rather than relying entirely on a single black spokesman (as his cousin Theodore had relied on Booker T. Washington), Franklin Roosevelt met freely with many black leaders and, although he gave none official authority, had what was termed a Black Cabinet. Although Roosevelt refused to alter the most significant oppressions of blacks, particularly in the South (he did nothing about lynching), he steadily increased the number of blacks on the federal payroll, especially in unskilled areas like the postal service. For blacks this truly was a New Deal.

And in still other ways Roosevelt's New Deal worked for good in mysterious ways. In the North, under the WPA, many painters, actors and writers, black and white, were hired to do "useless" artistic make-work. In the South, the FSA, in addition to improving the lot of the tenant farmers and sharecroppers that the AAA had ignored by offering fair credit and cooperative marketing, sent out photographers to record the lives of the people the FSA strove to assist. Those photographers followed the channel of the river that flowed northward. By 1941 they had produced an archive of 65,000 photographs, a pictorial history of people who, lacking literacy and the leisure time necessary to the keeping of written records, in a real sense lived outside the realm of traditional history. These were people who, from the point of view of most of America, had neither faces nor voices. The FSA gave them faces. Their voice was yet to come.

Nineteen forty. Germany invaded Norway, Denmark, Holland, Belgium and Luxembourg, and took Paris. A half-million refugee-immigrants reached America, adding to the 4.5 million aliens already here, including composers Schoenberg, Stravinsky and Bartok. American music was enriched by their presence and by that of the newly "discovered" Duke Ellington. And on March 1, American literature reached a turning point in its history, when Harper & Brothers published a first novel by a relatively unknown author named Richard Wright. On publication day the *New York Post* announced that the book, *Native Son*, deserved all the literary prizes. It quickly became a commercial phenomenon. it was a main selection of the Book-of-the-Month Club and over thirteen hundred club members requested it in the first week. It set a sales record for Harper—200,000 copies in less than three weeks. At the end of March, it was still selling 2,000 copies a day, and was number one on the best-seller list by April 1, ahead of John Steinbeck's *The Grapes of Wrath*. It continued to do well commercially, and in December, *Time* named it the most promising novel of the year. The kudos echoed for decades. In 1963, Irving Howe wrote that "The day *Native Son* appeared, American culture was changed forever."

Part of what made *Native Son* historically remarkable was the race of the author; Richard Wright was a black writer—certainly not the first America had heard of, or even the first to receive critical acclaim, but certainly the first to achieve such commercial and popular success in addition to critical acclaim. That success made Richard Wright America's first black literary celebrity, the possessor of unique wealth and fame. Excepting Joe Louis and Jesse Owens, he was probably the best-known black in white America—Jackie Robinson's big league debut was seven years away.

Wright's first book, *Uncle Tom's Children*, had been published by Harper in 1938. In its originally–published version, a collection of four novellas, *Uncle Tom's Children* graphically described the plight of blacks in the rural South, offering eloquent explanation of the Great Migration. When it appeared in 1938, it received the lavish praise of such critics as Malcolm Cowley, Alain Locke and Frederic T. March—the last compared Wright to Chekhov and intimated that he could win the Pulitzer Prize. Although he did not win the Pulitzer, on the strength of the book (and a recommendation from Eleanor Roosevelt), Wright did win a $2,500 Guggenheim Fellowship, with the aid of which he completed *Native Son*, a tragic melodrama about a young black migrant from the South who is immolated on a catherine wheel of violence after he accidentally kills the daughter of his white employer. And so with *Native Son's* publication, Wright in a sense completed a fictional chronicle of the Great Migration.

It was a story he was uniquely equipped to tell. For unlike other black writers—such as, for example, W. E. B. Du Bois, who was Northern born and classically educated—Richard Wright was a representative drop of the mighty migrant river which had flowed north from the fields of the Black Belt into the tenements of the Steel Belt. He was born near Natchez, Mississippi, in 1908. In

1927 he journeyed north to Chicago in the second wave of migration, responding to the mythology of the North: as he later wrote, his head was ''full of a hazy notion that life could be lived with dignity, that the personalities of others should not be violated, that men should be able to confront other men without fear or shame, and that if men were lucky in their living on earth they might win some redeeming meaning for their having struggled and suffered here beneath the stars.'' In Chicago, he pursued an exacting regimen of self-education, became involved with the Communist party (although he never actually joined) and worked in the post office. In 1937 he moved to New York to become the Harlem editor of the Communist *Daily Worker* and, eventually, an employee of the WPA's Federal Writers' Project.

Given his experience with the WPA, and the awesome success of *Native Son*, it was natural that in mid-1940 he should be asked to provide a text for a book to be published by the Viking Press, a selection of photographs from the archives of the Farm Credit Administration. In the summer of 1940, as *Native Son* dominated the best-seller lists, Wright began work on the text.

It is impossible to say what the editors at Viking expected the text to be like—probably they didn't care, as the name of Richard Wright on the cover was a guarantee that the book would be a success. Certainly they did not expect much, as the text was supposed to take up a mere twenty pages. But Wright became fascinated with telling a story which was very much his own story. Twenty pages quickly became more than fifty, as Wright, now able to avoid the luxuries of a secretary and a Dictaphone, went through as many as six revisions of each section. He delivered the manuscript in mid-July of 1941 and then withdrew it for still more revisions before allowing it at last to leave his hands.

Such rethinking and revision were not typical of Wright, who in his later career showed a tendency to release his work too soon, with disastrous results—indeed, his next project, an entire novel, was written in less than six months and, Wright's expectations to the contrary, totally rejected by the publisher in less than three. But with *Twelve Million Black Voices* he took his time, not only with the writing, but with the research. And not only with the kind of objective research that gave empirical and theoretical scope to the writing, but personal research. For to the writing of *Twelve Million Black Voices*, Richard Wright brought the findings from two sentimental journeys: one to Chicago, and one through the South.

When he visited Chicago, Wright was very much the hero returned. He purchased a house for his family and made the intellectual rounds. The research he did was objective, coming to a great extent from the files of a social worker named Horace Cayton. (It was in the course of brainstorming discussions with Cayton that Wright developed the idea that the forces that affected black life in America were different manifestations of property ownership—the "Lords of the Land" in the agrarian South and "Bosses of Buildings" in the industrial North.) But there was emotional strain in his life too—people who met him commented on an air of withdrawal and emotional fatigue, even social acidity.

But it was the trip to the South that was probably more significant. He entered the South in a state of emotional turmoil, recently separated from his new wife—they would soon divorce—and frustrated by his inability to settle down to a new novel. He entered too from an odd direction, from the south, from Mexico, where he had spent three months living in a ten-room villa and had been impressed with what he saw as a society where life was cheap but "where people of all races and colors live in harmony and without racial prejudices or theories of racial superiority. Whatever the accuracy of his observation, there is no doubt that it was a shock for him to cross the border into Texas, to ride to Natchez in the Jim Crow car. And it was a shock too for him to return, after a quarter century, to the place he had fled, to see his father for the first time in all those years, to confront the ironic fact that he was now separated involuntarily from that which he had separated himself voluntarily. "I discovered," he wrote, "that blood and race alone were not sufficient to knit a people together in a community of feeling. . . . I knew it was not the myth of blood but continued associations, shared ideals and kindred intentions that make a people one." This realization would add to *Twelve Million Black Voices* the theme of generational tension, which in turn gave the rather simplistic Marxist analysis of society a psychological depth. But if Wright would discover in Natchez how much he had changed, he would be reminded on his next stop, Chapel Hill, North Carolina, how much the South had not. Although he was in Chapel Hill to work on the stage version of *Native Son*, the fact that he was a celebrated author did not impress the neighbors of his collaborator, Paul Green; they made it quite clear that they did not welcome the presence of a black in their community. Little wonder, as Ralph Ellison observed, "he came back very disturbed."

But if his experiences in research disturbed him, the experience of looking at the photographs themselves must have produced emotions so deep and complex that they can have no simple name. For while the sum of his recent experiences had shown him exactly where and what he was in the world, the faces in the photographs showed him clearly where and what he could have been. Each of the faces in the FSA photographs could easily have been his face, perhaps had been. The face of the black boy at the end of section one could have been the face of Wright himself before he made his Exodus to the North. The face of the lynched man could have been his had he not left in time. The face of the sharecropper could have been his had he not left but managed to avoid the rope. The face of the black youth in his fancy clothes could have been his had he not been a serious person, a man with a dream. There, but for the grace of God was Richard Wright.

In all his writings, both before and after *Native Son*, Wright tended to respond to existing artifacts—newspaper stories, psychological studies and so forth. Here, for the first and perhaps only time in his career, he responded to images rather than words, to unstructured ideas. And so perhaps it is not surprising that the text of *Twelve Million Black Voices* has a lyrical power, an impressionistic rather than logical structure, a power of a type different than that achieved in any of the work he was able to publish in the forties. It was a fluid power, a clarity of expression that he would not achieve again until the mid-fifties, very near the end of his career. Whatever their virtues, *Uncle Tom's Children, Native Son* and his next great success, his autobiography, *Black Boy*, were works of calculation and retrospection, written in a voice of reasoned protest. But in *Twelve Million Black Voices* Richard Wright spoke in a voice of passion. In *Twelve Million Black Voices* Richard Wright sang.

It is perhaps too romantic to suggest that the voice in which he wrote was, as the artistic use of the first person plural implies, not Wright's voice but that of his people. But it is only accurate to say that in using ''we'' Wright was not involved in mere artistic conceit. He had followed the ebb and flow of the river of black life in a way that no other writer of the day had. He alone had the right to say ''we.'' And while it may be romantic it nevertheless seems that the voice Wright used to tell this story—his story—was a special voice. So it surely seems now. For among all the works of Richard Wright, *Twelve Million Black Voices* stands out as a work of poetry, of passion, of lyricism and of love.

DAVID BRADLEY

Foreword

THIS TEXT, while purporting to render a broad picture of the processes of Negro life in the United States, intentionally does not include in its considerations those areas of Negro life which comprise the so-called "talented tenth," or the isolated islands of mulatto leadership which are still to be found in many parts of the South, or the growing and influential Negro middle-class professional and business men of the North who have, for the past thirty years or more, formed a sort of liaison corps between the whites and the blacks. Their exclusion from these pages does not imply any invidious judgment, nor does it stem from any desire to underestimate their progress and contributions; they are omitted in an effort to simplify a depiction of a complex movement of a debased feudal folk toward a twentieth-century urbanization.

This text assumes that those few Negroes who have lifted themselves, through personal strength, talent, or luck, above the lives of their fellow-blacks—like single fishes that leap and flash for a split second above the surface of the sea—are but fleeting exceptions to that vast, tragic school that swims below in the depths, against the current, silently and heavily, struggling against the waves of vicissitudes that spell a common fate. It is not, however, to celebrate or exalt the plight of the humble folk who swim in the depths that I select the conditions of their lives as examples of normality, but rather to seize upon that which is qualitative and abiding in Negro experience, to place within full and constant view the collective humanity whose triumphs and defeats are shared by the majority, whose gains in security mark an advance in the level of consciousness attained by the broad masses in their costly and tortuous upstream journey.

This text, therefore, accepts as basic and centrally historical those materials of Negro life identified with the countless black millions who made up the bulk of the slave population during the seventeenth, eighteenth, and nineteenth centuries; those teeming black millions who endured the physical and spiritual ravages of serfdom; those legions of nameless blacks who felt the shock and hope of sudden emancipation; those terrified black folk who withstood the brutal wrath of the Ku Klux Klan, and who fled the cotton and tobacco plantations to seek refuge in northern and southern cities coincident with the decline of the cotton culture of the Old South.

The majority of the concepts and interpretations upon which I have relied most heavily in the assembling and writing of this text came from *The Negro Family in the United States* by E. Franklin Frazier; *Rum, Romance and Rebellion* by Charles W. Taussig; *Sharecroppers All* by Arthur Raper and Ira De A. Reid; *History of the American Negro People, 1619–1918* by Elizabeth Lawson; "Urbanism as a Way of Life" (from the *American Journal of Sociology,* Volume XLIV, Number 1, July 1938) by Louis Wirth; and *Black Workers and the New Unions* by Horace R. Cayton and George S. Mitchell.

I take this opportunity to extend my thanks and appreciation to Mr. Horace R. Cayton, director of the Good Shepherd Community Center of Chicago, for his making available his immense files of materials on urban life among Negroes and, above all, for the advice and guidance which made sections of this book possible.

RICHARD WRIGHT

Contents

1.

Our Strange Birth

EACH DAY when you see us black folk upon the dusty land of the farms or upon the hard pavement of the city streets, you usually take us for granted and think you know us, but our history is far stranger than you suspect, and we are not what we seem.

Our outward guise still carries the old familiar aspect which three hundred years of oppression in America have given us, but beneath the garb of the black laborer, the black cook, and the black elevator operator lies an uneasily tied knot of pain and hope whose snarled strands converge from many points of time and space.

We millions of black folk who live in this land were born into Western civilization of a weird and paradoxical birth. The lean, tall, blond men of England, Holland, and Denmark, the dark, short, nervous men of France, Spain, and Portugal, men whose blue and gray and brown eyes glinted with the light of the future, denied our human personalities, tore us from our native soil, weighted our legs with chains, stacked us like cord-wood in the foul holes of clipper ships, dragged us across thousands of miles of ocean, and hurled us into another land, strange and hostile, where for a second time we felt the slow, painful process of a new birth amid conditions harsh and raw.

The immemorial stars must have gazed down in amazement at the lowly of England and Europe, who, with hearts full of hope, pushed out to sea to urge rebellion against tyranny and then straightway became engaged in the slave trade, in the buying and selling of our human bodies. And those same stars must have smiled when, following the War of Independence, the Lords of the Land in the South relaxed their rigid slave code ever so little to square their guilty conscience with the lofty ideals of the rights of man for which they had fought and died; but never did they relax their code so much as to jeopardize their claim of ownership of us.

Our captors were hard men, brutal men; yet they held locked somewhere within their hearts the fertile seeds that were to sprout into a new world culture, that were to blossom into a higher human consciousness. Escaping from the fetid medieval dens, angrily doffing the burial sheets of feudal religion, and flushed with a new and noble concept of life, of its inherent dignity, of its unlimited possibilities, of its natural worth, these men leaped upon the road of progress; and their leap was the windfall of our tragedy. Their excessive love of life wove a deadly web of slavery that snared our naked feet. Their sense of the possibility of building a more humane world brought devastation and despair to our pointed huts on the long, tan shores of Africa. We were an unlucky people; the very contours and harbors of our native land conspired against our freedom. The coastline of our Africa was long and flat and easy to invade; we had no mountains to serve as natural forts from behind which we could fight and stave off the slave traders.

We had our own civilization in Africa before we were captured and carried off to this land. You may smile when we call the way of life we lived in Africa "civilization," but in numerous respects the culture of many of our tribes was equal to that of the lands from which the slave captors came. We smelted iron, danced, made music, and recited folk poems; we sculptured, worked in glass, spun cotton and wool, wove baskets and cloth; we invented a medium of exchange, mined silver and gold, made pottery and cutlery; we fashioned tools and utensils of brass, bronze, ivory, quartz, and granite; we had our own literature, our own systems of law, religion, medicine, science, and education; we painted in color upon rocks; we raised cattle, sheep, and goats; we planted and harvested grain—in short, centuries before the Romans ruled, we lived as men.

Our humanity, however, did not save us; the New England Puritans and the imperialists of Europe erected the traffic in our bodies into the "big business" of the eighteenth century, and but few industries the world has ever known have yielded higher profits. There were "tricks of the trade" then as now; the slave traders, operators of fleets of stench-ridden sailing vessels, were comparable to our contemporary "captains of industry" and "tycoons of finance," and the Union Jack and the Stars and Stripes fluttered from the masts of men-of-war as the ensign of protection for "free trade" in our bodies. It was mainly the kings of vast rum distilleries who owned the ships that scoured the seven seas in search of our bodies. Jew as well as Gentile took part in these voyages of plunder. Nation waged war against nation for the right to buy and sell us, just as today they fight for "markets and raw materials." To Africa the traders brought rum and swapped it to corrupt chiefs for our bodies; we were then taken to the colonies, the West Indies, Cuba, and Brazil and used as currency to buy molasses; the molasses in turn was taken to the distilleries of New England and bartered for rum, which formed the basis for another slave voyage.

The slave ships, equipped for long voyages, were floating brothels for the slave traders of the seventeenth and eighteenth centuries. Bound by heavy chains, we gazed impassively upon the lecherous crew members as they vented the pent-up bestiality of their starved sex lives upon our sisters and wives. This was a peculiar practice which, as the years flowed past, grew into a clandestine but well-established institution which the owners of cotton and tobacco plantations upheld, and which today, in large measure, accounts for the widespread mulatto population in the United States. Indeed, there were slave-breeding farms. Slaves were valuable; cotton meant cash, and each able-bodied slave could be depended upon to produce at least 5000 pounds of cotton each year.

The *Mayflower's* nameless sister ship, presumably a Dutch vessel, which stole into the harbor of Jamestown in 1619 and unloaded her human cargo of 20 of us, was but the first such ship to touch the shores of this New World, and her arrival signalized what was to be our trial for centuries to come. More than 14,000,000 of us were brought to America alone. For every 100 of us who survived the terrible journey across the Atlantic, the so-called "middle passage" of these voyages, 400 of us perished. During three hundred years—the seventeenth, eighteenth, and nineteenth centuries—more than 100,000,000 of us were torn from our African homes. Until the dawn of the nineteenth century, slavery was legal the world over.

Laid out spoon-fashion on the narrow decks of sailing ships, we were transported to this New World so closely packed that the back of the head of one of us nestled between the legs of another. Sometimes 720 of us were jammed into a space 20 feet wide, 120 feet long, and 5 feet high. Week after week we would lie there, tortured and gasping, as the ship heaved and tossed over the waves. In the summer, down in the suffocating depths of those ships, on an eight- or ten-week voyage, we would go crazed for lack of air and water, and in the morning the crew of the ship would discover many of us dead, clutching in rigor mortis at the throats of our friends, wives, or children.

During the seventeenth century, to protect themselves against the overwhelming influx of us, some governments launched numerous men-of-war to track down and seize the slave ships. We captives did not know whether to feel dread or joy when a man-of-war was sighted, for the captain would command that a few of us be pitched alive into the sea as moral bait to compel the captain of the pursuing ship to desist from his duty. Every mile or so one of us would be bound fast to a cask or spar and tossed overboard with the hope that the sight of our forlorn struggle against the sea would stir such compassion in the heart of the captain of the man-of-war that he would abandon pursuit, thereby enabling the slave ships to escape.

At other times, when we were sick, we were thrown alive into the sea and the captain, pilgrim of progress, would studiously enter into the ship's log two words that would balance all earthly accounts: "jettisoned cargo."

At still other times we went on hunger strikes; but the time allotted us to starve to death was often too short, and the ship would arrive in port before we had outwitted the slave traders. The more ambitious slavers possessed instruments with which to pry our teeth apart and feed us forcibly. Whenever we could we leaped into the sea.

To quench all desire for mutiny in us, they would sometimes decapitate a few of us and impale our black heads upon the tips of the spars, just as years later they impaled our heads upon the tips of pine trees for miles along the dusty highways of Dixie to frighten us into obedience.

Captivity under Christendom blasted our lives, disrupted our families, reached down into the personalities of each one of us and destroyed the very images and symbols which had guided our minds and feelings in the effort to live. Our folkways and folk tales, which had once given meaning and sanction to our actions, faded from consciousness. Our gods were dead and answered us no more. The trauma of leaving our African home, the suffering of the long middle passage, the thirst, the hunger, the horrors of the slave ship—all these hollowed us out, numbed us, stripped us, and left only physiological urges, the feelings of fear and fatigue.

Against the feudal background of denials of love and happiness, the trade in our bodies bred god-like men who exalted honor, enthroned impulse, glorified aspiration, celebrated individuality, and fortified the human heart to strive against the tyrannical forms of nature and to bend obstreperous materials closer to a mold that would slake human desire. As time elapsed, these new men seized upon the unfolding discoveries of science and invention, and, figuratively, their fingers became hot as fire and hard as steel. Literature, art, music, and philosophy set their souls aflame with a desire for the new mode of living that had come into the world. Exploration opened wide the entire surface of the earth as a domain of adventure. Window glass, drugs to dull pain, printing presses, larger ships, bigger and more powerful guns—these and a thousand other commodities began to spread across the area of man's living and give it a new quality. Never before had human life on earth felt more confident; human feelings grew sensitive and complex, and human sentiment, pouring from the newly released human organism, wrapped itself about the whole world, each man and object in it, creating an all-powerful atmosphere of ambition and passion in which we black slaves were the main objects of exploitation.

Sustained by an incredible hope such as the world had never felt before, the slavers continued to snatch us by the millions from our native African soil to be used as tools to till the tobacco, rice, sugar-cane, and cotton plantations; they built powerful empires, replete with authority and comfort, and, as a protecting superstructure, they spun tight ideological webs of their right to domination. Daily these eager men slashed off the rotting trappings of feudal life, a life which for centuries had endowed man with a metaphysical worth, rank, use, and order; and, in its stead, they launched the foundations of a new dispensation to prove that man could step beyond the boundaries of ignorance and superstition and live by reason. And they shackled millions of us to labor for them, to give them the instrumentalities.

But as we blacks toiled, millions of poor free whites, against whom our slave labor was pitted, were rendered indigent and helpless. The gold of slave-grown cotton concentrated the political power of the Old South in the hands of a few Lords of the Land, and the poor whites decreased in number as we blacks increased. To protect their delicately balanced edifice of political power, the Lords of the Land proceeded to neutralize the strength of us blacks and the growing restlessness of the poor whites by dividing and ruling us, by inciting us against one another. But, complementing this desire for safety, there was the growth of the hunger for more wealth, and the Lords of the Land increased their importations of us, and in turn we blacks continued to squeeze the poor whites to lower levels of living. Fear became the handmaid of cotton culture, spreading and deepening; but the slave ships sailed on, bringing thousands of us yearly to the New World.

The beginning of the eighteenth century marked the rise of a fully developed anti-slavery sentiment in the North. Tardily, the French Revolution captured to some degree the imagination of the New England Puritans, and again there sounded a passionate, humanitarian belief in the rights of man; and, overlapping this, there came the religious exhortations of the Quakers, with their mystical belief in the Golden Rule. And we black tools responded as fervently as did the rest of mankind to the call of Liberty, Equality, and Fraternity, to the expressed conviction that all men were equal in the sight of God. Fury swept the hearts of the Lords of the Land who heard spilling from the thick, black lips of their tools the first broken syllables of freedom, the first stammered assertions of manhood. The foundations of their world trembled and they turned their eyes to God, seized whips, knives, or guns, and rushed forth, bellowing to set aright the order of the universe.

In the latter part of the eighteenth century, however, the conduct of most of the Lords of the Land began to alter toward us. To evade the prevailing Christian injunction that all baptized men are free, and to check our growing record of revolt, they culled from the Bible a thousand quotable verses admonishing us slaves to be true to our masters. Thereupon they felt that

17

they had squared conscience with practice, and they extended Christian salvation to us without granting the boon of freedom. This dual attitude, compounded of a love of gold and God, was the beginning of America's paternalistic code toward her black maid, her black industrial worker, her black stevedore, her black dancer, her black waiter, her black sharecropper; it was a code of casual cruelty, of brutal kindness, of genial despotism, a code which has survived, grown, spread, and congealed into a national tradition that dominates, in small or large measure, all black and white relations throughout the nation until this day.

The black maid

The black industrial worker

The black stevedore

The black dancer

The black waiter

The black sharecropper

How did this paradoxical amalgam of love and cruelty come to be? Well, men are many and each has his work to do. A division of labor among men, splitting them up into groups and classes, enables whole segments of populations to be so influenced by their material surroundings that they see but a little phase of the complex process of their lives and the whole is obscured from them, thereby affording them the unfortunate opportunity to move and work at cross-purposes with one another, even though in their hearts they may feel that they are engaged in a crusade of common hope.

So our bent backs continued to give design and order to the fertile plantations. Stately governmental structures and vast palatial homes were reared by our black hands to reflect the genteel glory of the new age. And the Lords of the Land created and administered laws in the belief that *their* God ruled in Heaven, that He sanctioned this new day. After they had amassed mountains of wealth, they compared the wretchedness of our lives with the calm gentility of theirs and felt that they were truly the favored of God. The lyrical mantle of prayer and hymn, accordingly, justified and abetted our slavery; and whenever we murmured against the degradation of the plantation, the Lords of the Land acted against us with whips and hate to protect their God-sanctioned civilization.

Our black bodies were good tools that had to be kept efficient for toil. Therefore, when schools were built, it was decreed that we must not partake of the teaching in them. When praises were sung to God, it was decided that we must not lift our voices in common hymn. Time and again we rose and struck angrily for freedom; sometimes we revolted in two's and three's; at other times we rose by the thousands, trying to break through the white wall that hemmed us in.

Convinced now at last of peril, the Lords of the Land began to drape their possessions in the protective hues of rationalism, to write and preach of their humanity and justice, but they found that the lash and the mob were needed to keep their positions of power, and soon these twin serpents of terror were organically entwined about the columns of legal government.

The eyes of the Lords of the Land grew challenging; but, blinded by the glittering prize they sought to keep, they could not detect the stealthy forces at work in the world, forces which were destined to wreck their empire and disperse us black men like whirling atoms upon the face of the earth.

The hope which had lured millions of restless men into the New World still lived precariously in many hearts, untouched by the fever of possession and the seduction of power. From English and Yankee brains there came in quick succession the spinning jenny, the spinning mule, and the application of steam power. There began to crawl across the landscape lumbering machines that magically threatened to turn millions of our black fingers idle. And the generous earth, once so green and so new, began to rot the seed and stunt the plant, forcing the Lords of the Land, in their search for new soil, to migrate westward, where they clashed with free men to whom the slave ethic was useless and obnoxious.

Eastern industry, which had begun to flood the nation with commodities, was owned by men who wielded a new type of authority. Free white labor of the North and West built thousands upon thousands of buildings—dwellings, shops, factories, mills, and foundries—and the Bosses of the Buildings, the bankers, foresaw that the day was coming when we slaves would not be worth the food we ate. These men grew alarmed over the fate of their nation and over their own ultimate racial identity in face of the black tide of us who were being poured out of the clipper ships.

The opinion of the nation divided into two opposing constellations: a world of machines and a world of slaves. Two groups of leaders sprang up: the Bosses of the Buildings and the Lords of the Land. As the full consequences of the two divergent ways of life became manifest, millions began an impassioned questioning of the basis of the ideas which they had sought to make operative in the New World. A small minority, both north and south, felt outraged at a system of human bondage that nullified all they had so ardently striven to build, and many sensitive men grew violent against *all* government and went up and down the land propounding the principles of passive resistance and civil disobedience.

In an atmosphere of such tension, the whites began to distrust each other. Therefore, when the Bosses of the Buildings suggested that we blacks be deported and colonized, the Lords of the Land rose and threatened to resort to a wholesale breeding of slaves in order not to be deprived of our living bodies. And, on the other hand, when the Lords of the Land, afraid of our growing numbers and increasing rebelliousness, suggested that the entire nation be taxed to raise money to deport us, the Bosses of the Buildings declared that such a course would destroy the capital of the nation, stifle productivity, and crush the poor whites, who were already being smothered in the slave atmosphere. But as we blacks continued to multiply and spread, the Lords of the Land sought to distribute us on the plantations so that our population would never exceed that of the whites or grow so great in any one area as to constitute an insurrectionary danger.

To enjoy a spell more of time in their cool mansions, the majority of the Lords of the Land disciplined the animal panic in their hearts and decided to hang on; they declared their independence, and war was waged for new lands to expand in, for the right to import more of us to raise cotton. And the Bosses of the Buildings, eager to manufacture and sell their commodities, stood against them in four years of battle to protect themselves, their future, and their hope of an industrial civilization.

We were freed because of a gnawing of some obscure sense of guilt, because of a cloudy premonition of impending disaster, because of a soil becoming rapidly impoverished, because of the hunger for fresh land, because of the new logic of life that came in the wake of clanking machines —it was all these things, and not the strength of moral ideals alone, that lessened the grip of the Lords of the Land upon us.

Reasons of being freed

We black men and women in America today, as we look back upon scenes of rapine, sacrifice, and death, seem to be children of a devilish aberration, descendants of an interval of nightmare in history, fledglings of a period of amnesia on the part of men who once dreamed a great dream and forgot.

2.

Inheritors of Slavery

THE WORD "NEGRO," the term by which, orally or in print, we black folk in the United States are usually designated, is not really a name at all nor a description, but a psychological island whose objective form is the most unanimous fiat in all American history; a fiat buttressed by popular and national tradition, and written down in many state and city statutes; a fiat which artificially and arbitrarily defines, regulates, and limits in scope of meaning the vital contours of our lives, and the lives of our children and our children's children.

This island, within whose confines we live, is anchored in the feelings of millions of people, and is situated in the midst of the sea of white faces we meet each day; and, by and large, as three hundred years of time has borne our nation into the twentieth century, its rocky boundaries have remained unyielding to the waves of our hope that dash against it.

The steep cliffs of this island are manifest, on the whole, in the conduct of whites toward us hour by hour, a conduct which tells us that we possess no rights commanding respect, that we have no claim to pursue happiness in our own fashion, that our progress toward civilization constitutes an insult, that our behavior must be kept firmly within an orbit branded as inferior, that we must be compelled to labor at the behest of others, that as a group we are owned by the whites, and that manliness on our part warrants instant reprisal.

Three hundred years are a long time for millions of folk like us to be held in such subjection, so long a time that perhaps scores of years will have to pass before we shall be able to express what this slavery has done to us, for our personalities are still numb from its long shocks; and, as the numbness leaves our souls, we shall yet have to feel and give utterance to the full pain we shall inherit.

More than one-half of us black folk in the United States are tillers of the soil, and three-fourths of those of us who till the soil are sharecroppers and day laborers.

The land we till is beautiful, with red and black and brown clay, with fresh and hungry smells, with pine trees and palm trees, with rolling hills and swampy delta—an unbelievably fertile land, bounded on the north by the states of Pennsylvania, Ohio, Illinois, and Indiana, on the south by the Gulf of Mexico, on the west by the Mississippi River, and on the east by the Atlantic Ocean.

Our southern springs are filled with quiet noises and scenes of growth. Apple buds laugh into blossom. Honeysuckles creep up the sides of houses. Sunflowers nod in the hot fields. From mossy tree to mossy tree—oak, elm, willow, aspen, sycamore, dogwood, cedar, walnut, ash, and hickory—bright green leaves jut from a million branches to form an awning that tries to shield and shade the earth. Blue and pink kites of small boys sail in the windy air.

In summer the magnolia trees fill the countryside with sweet scent for long miles. Days are slumberous, and the skies are high and thronged with clouds that ride fast. At midday the sun blazes and bleaches the soil. Butter-flies flit through the heat; wasps sing their sharp, straight lines; birds fluff and flounce, piping in querulous joy. Nights are covered with canopies sometimes blue and sometimes black, canopies that sag low with ripe and nervous stars. The throaty boast of frogs momentarily drowns out the call and counter-call of crickets.

In autumn the land is afire with color. Red and brown leaves lift and flutter dryly, becoming entangled in the stiff grass and cornstalks. Cotton is picked and ginned; cane is crushed and its juice is simmered down into molasses; yams are grubbed out of the clay; hogs are slaughtered and cured in lingering smoke; corn is husked and ground into meal. At twilight the sky is full of wild geese winging ever southward, and bats jerk through the air. At night the winds blow free.

In winter the forests resound with the bite of steel axes eating into tall trees as men gather wood for the leaden days of cold. The guns of hunters snap and crack. Long days of rain come, and our swollen creeks rush to

LIBRARY
COLBY-SAWYER COLLEGE
NEW LONDON, NH 03257

join a hundred rivers that wash across the land and make great harbors where they feed the gulf or the sea. Occasionally the rivers leap their banks and leave new thick layers of silt to enrich the earth, and then the look of the land is garish, bleak, suffused with a first-day stillness, strangeness, and awe.

But whether in spring or summer or autumn or winter, time slips past us remorselessly, and it is hard to tell of the iron that lies beneath the surface of our quiet, dull days.

To paint the picture of how we live on the tobacco, cane, rice, and cotton plantations is to compete with mighty artists: the movies, the radio, the newspapers, the magazines, and even the Church. They have painted one picture: charming, idyllic, romantic; but we live another: full of the fear of the Lords of the Land, bowing and grinning when we meet white faces, toiling from sun to sun, living in unpainted wooden shacks that sit casually and insecurely upon the red clay.

In the main we are different from other folk in that, when an impulse moves us, when we are caught in the throes of inspiration, when we are moved to better our lot, we do not ask ourselves: "Can we do it?" but: "Will they let us do it?" Before we black folk can move, we must first look into the white man's mind to see what is there, to see what he is thinking, and the white man's mind is a mind that is always changing.

In general there are three classes of men above us: the Lords of the Land —operators of the plantations; the Bosses of the Buildings—the owners of industry; and the vast numbers of poor white workers—our immediate competitors in the daily struggle for bread. The Lords of the Land hold sway over the plantations and over us; the Bosses of the Buildings lend money and issue orders to the Lords of the Land. The Bosses of the Buildings feed upon the Lords of the Land, and the Lords of the Land feed upon the 5,000,000 landless poor whites and upon us, throwing to the poor whites the scant solace of filching from us 4,000,000 landless blacks what the poor whites themselves are cheated of in this elaborate game.

Back of this tangled process is a long history. When the Emancipation Proclamation was signed, there were some 4,000,000 of us black folk stranded and bewildered upon the land which we had tilled under compulsion for two and a half centuries. Sundered suddenly from the only relationship with Western civilization we had been allowed to form since our captivity, our personalities blighted by two hundred and fifty years of servitude, and eager to hold our wives and husbands and children together in family units, some of us turned back to the same Lords of the Land who had held us as slaves and begged for work, resorted to their advice; and there began for us a new kind of bondage: sharecropping.

Glad to be free, some of us drifted and gave way to every vagary of impulse that swept through us, being held in the line of life only by the necessity to work and eat. Confined for centuries to the life of the cotton field, many of us possessed no feelings of family, home, community, race, church, or progress. We could scarcely believe that we were free, and our restlessness and incessant mobility were our naïve way of testing that freedom. Just as a kitten stretches and yawns after a long sleep, so thousands of us tramped from place to place for the sheer sake of moving, looking, wondering, landless upon the land. Arkansas, Missouri, Tennessee, Kentucky, North Carolina, South Carolina, Louisiana, Alabama, Mississippi, Georgia, Virginia, and West Virginia became the home states of us freed blacks.

In 1890 many white people predicted that we black folk would perish in a competitive world; but in spite of this we left the land and kept afloat, wandering from Natchez to New Orleans, from Mobile to Montgomery, from Macon to Jacksonville, from Birmingham to Chattanooga, from Nashville to Louisville, from Memphis to Little Rock—laboring in the sawmills, in the turpentine camps, on the road jobs; working for men who did not care if we lived or died, but who did not want their business enterprises to suffer for lack of labor. During the first decade of the twentieth century, more than one and three-quarter millions of us abandoned the plantations upon which we had been born; more than a million of us roamed the states of the South and the remainder of us drifted north.

Our women fared easier than we men during the early days of freedom; on the whole their relationship to the world was more stable than ours. Their authority was supreme in most of our families inasmuch as many of them had worked in the "Big Houses" of the Lords of the Land and had learned manners, had been taught to cook, sew, and nurse. During slave days they did not always belong to us, for the Lords of the Land often took them for their pleasure. When a gang of us was sold from one plantation to another, our wives would sometimes be kept by the Lords of the Land and we men would have to mate with whatever slave girl we chanced upon. Because of their enforced intimacy with the Lords of the Land, many of our women, after they were too old to work, were allowed to remain in the slave cabins to tend generations of black children. They enjoyed a status denied us men, being called "Mammy"; and through the years they became symbols of motherhood, retaining in their withered bodies the burden of our folk wisdom, reigning as arbiters in our domestic affairs until we men were freed and had moved to cities where cash-paying jobs enabled us to become the heads of our own families.

The economic and political power of the South is not held in our hands; we do not own banks, iron and steel mills, railroads, office buildings, ships, wharves, or power plants. There are some few of us who operate small grocery stores, barber shops, rooming houses, burial societies, and undertaking establishments. But none of us owns any of the basic industries that shape the course of the South, such as mining, lumber, textiles, oil, transportation, or electric power. So, in the early spring, when the rains have ceased and the ground is ready for plowing, we present ourselves to the Lords of the Land and ask to make a crop. We sign a contract—usually our contracts are oral—which allows us to keep one-half of the harvest after all debts are paid. If we have worked upon these plantations before, we are legally bound to plant, tend, and harvest another crop. If we should escape to the city to avoid paying our mounting debts, white policemen track us down and ship us back to the plantation.

The Lords of the Land assign us ten or fifteen acres of soil already bled of its fertility through generations of abuse. They advance us one mule, one plow, seed, tools, fertilizer, clothing, and food, the main staples of which are fat hog meat, coarsely ground corn meal, and sorghum molasses. If we have been lucky the year before, maybe we have saved a few dollars to tide us through the fall months, but spring finds us begging an "advance" —credit—from the Lords of the Land.

From now on the laws of Queen Cotton rule our lives. (Contrary to popular assumption, cotton is a *queen,* not a king. Kings are dictatorial; cotton is not only dictatorial but self-destructive, an imperious woman in the throes of constant childbirth, a woman who is driven by her greedy passion to bear endless bales of cotton, though she well knows that she will die if she continues to give birth to her fleecy children!) If we black folk had only to work to feed the Lords of the Land, to supply delicacies for their tables—as did the slaves of old for their masters—our degradation upon the plantations would not have been the harshest form of human servitude the world has ever known. But we had to raise cotton to clothe

the world; cotton meant money, and money meant power and authority and prestige. To plant vegetables for our tables was often forbidden, for raising a garden narrowed the area to be planted in cotton. The world demanded cotton, and the Lords of the Land ordered more acres to be planted—planted right up to our doorsteps!—and the ritual of Queen Cotton became brutal and bloody.

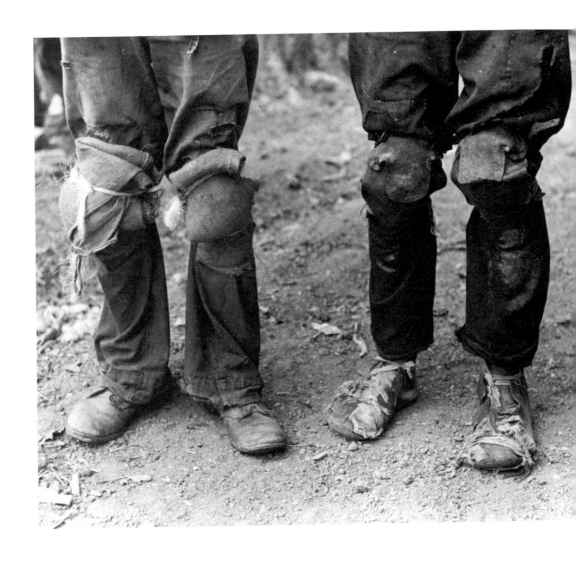

The laws of Queen Cotton rule our lives

Because they feel that they cannot trust us, the Lords of the Land assign a "riding boss" to go from cotton patch to cotton patch and supervise our work. We pay for the cost of this supervision out of our share of the harvest; we pay interest on the cost of the supplies which the Lords of the Land advance to us; and, because illness and death, rain and sun, boll weevil and storms, are hazards which might work to the detriment of the cotton crop, we agree to pay at harvest a "time price," a sum payable in cotton, corn, or cane, which the Lords of the Land charge us to cover a probable loss on their investment in us.

We who have followed the plow in this fashion have developed a secret life and language of our own. When we were first brought here from our innumerable African tribes, each of us spoke the language of his tribe. But the Lords of the Land decreed that we must be distributed upon the plantations so that no two of us who spoke a common tongue would be thrown together, lest we plot rebellion. So they shackled one slave to another slave of an alien tribe. Our eyes would look wistfully into the face of a fellow-victim of slavery, but we could say no word to him. Though we could hear, we were deaf; though we could speak, we were dumb!

We stole words from the grudging lips of the Lords of the Land, who did not want us to know too many of them or their meaning. And we charged this meager horde of stolen sounds with all the emotions and longings we had; we proceeded to build our language in inflections of voice, through tonal variety, by hurried speech, in honeyed drawls, by rolling our eyes, by flourishing our hands, by assigning to common, simple words new meanings, meanings which enabled us to speak of revolt in the actual presence of the Lords of the Land without their being aware! Our secret language extended our understanding of what slavery meant and gave us the freedom to speak to our brothers in captivity; we polished our new words, caressed them, gave them new shape and color, a new order and tempo, until, though they were the words of the Lords of the Land, they became *our* words, *our* language.

The steady impact of the plantation system upon our lives created new types of behavior and new patterns of psychological reaction, welding us together into a separate unity with common characteristics of our own. We strove each day to maintain that kind of external behavior that would best allay the fear and hate of the Lords of the Land, and over a period of years this dual conduct became second nature to us and we found in it a degree of immunity from daily oppression. Even when a white man asked us an innocent question, some unconscious part of us would listen closely, not only to the obvious words, but also to the intonations of voice that indicated what kind of answer he wanted; and, automatically, we would determine whether an affirmative or negative reply was expected, and we would answer, not in terms of objective truth, but in terms of what the white man wished to hear.

If a white man stopped a black on a southern road and asked: "Say, there, boy! It's one o'clock, isn't it?" the black man would answer: "Yessuh."

If the white man asked: "Say, it's not one o'clock, is it, boy?" the black man would answer: "Nawsuh."

And if the white man asked: "It's ten miles to Memphis, isn't it, boy?" the black man would answer: "Yessuh."

And if the white man asked: "It isn't ten miles to Memphis, is it, boy?" the black man would answer: "Nawsuh."

Always we said what we thought the whites wanted us to say.

So our years pass within the web of a system we cannot beat. Years of fat meat and corn meal and sorghum molasses, years of plowing and hoeing and picking, years of sun and wind and rain—these are the years that do with us what they will, that form our past, shape our present, and loom ahead as the outline of our future.

Most of the flogging and lynchings occur at harvest time, when fruit hangs heavy and ripe, when the leaves are red and gold, when nuts fall from the trees, when the earth offers its best. The thought of harvest steals upon us with a sense of an inescapable judgment. It is time now to settle accounts with the Lords of the Land, to divide the crops and pay old debts, and we are afraid. We have never grown used to confronting the Lords of the Land when the last of the cotton is ginned and baled, for we know beforehand that we have lost yet another race with time, that we are deeper in debt. When word reaches us that the Lords of the Land are bent over the big books down at the plantation commissary, we lower our eyes, shake our heads, and mutter:

> *A naught's a naught,*
> *Five's a figger;*
> *All for the white man,*
> *None for the nigger....*

If the Lord of the Land for whom we are working happens to be a foreigner who came to the United States to escape oppression in Europe, and who has taken to the native way of cheating us, we spit and mutter:

> Red, white, and blue,
> Your daddy was a Jew,
> Your ma's a dirty dago,
> Now what the hell is you?...

And after we have divided the crops we are still entangled as deeply as ever in this hateful web of cotton culture. We are older; our bodies are weaker; our families are larger; our clothes are in rags; we are still in debt; and, worst of all, we face another year that holds even less hope than the one we have just endured. We know that this is not right, and dark thoughts take possession of our minds. We know that to tread this mill is to walk in days of slow death. When alone, we stand and look out over the green, rolling fields and wonder why it is that living here is so hard. Everything seems to whisper of the possibility of happiness, of satisfying experiences; but somehow happiness and satisfaction never come into our lives. The land upon which we live holds a promise, but the promise fades with the passing seasons.

And we know that if we protest we will be called "bad niggers." The Lords of the Land will preach the doctrine of "white supremacy" to the poor whites who are eager to form mobs. In the midst of general hysteria they will seize one of us—it does not matter who, the innocent or guilty—and, as a token, a naked and bleeding body will be dragged through the dusty streets. The mobs will make certain that our token-death is known throughout the quarters where we black folk live. Our bodies will be swung by ropes from the limbs of trees, will be shot at and mutilated.

And we cannot fight back; we have no arms; we cannot vote; and the law is white. There are no black policemen, black justices of the peace, black judges, black juries, black jailers, black mayors, or black men anywhere in the government of the South. The Ku Klux Klan attacks us in a thousand ways, driving our boys and girls off the jobs in the cities and keeping us who live on the land from protesting or asking too many questions.

The law is white

This is the way the Lords of the Land keep their power. For them life is a continuous victory; for us it is simply trouble in the land. Fear is with us always, and in those areas where we black men equal or outnumber the whites fear is at its highest. Two streams of life flow through the South, a black stream and a white stream, and from day to day we live in the atmosphere of a war that never ends. Even when the sprawling fields are drenched in peaceful sunshine, it is war. When we grub at the clay with our hoes, it is war. When we sleep, it is war. When we are awake, it is war. When one of us is born, he enters one of the warring regiments of the South. When there are days of peace, it is a peace born of a victory over us; and when there is open violence, it is when we are trying to push back the encroachments of the Lords of the Land.

Sometimes, fleetingly, like a rainbow that comes and vanishes in its coming, the wan faces of the poor whites make us think that perhaps we can join our hands with them and lift the weight of the Lords of the Land off our backs. But, before new meanings can bridge the chasm that has been long created between us, the poor whites are warned by the Lords of the Land that they must cast their destiny with their own color, that to make common cause with us is to threaten the foundations of civilization. Fear breeds in our hearts until each poor white face begins to look like the face of an enemy soldier. We learn that almost all white men feel it is their duty to see that we do not go beyond the prescribed boundaries. And so both of us, the poor black and the poor white, are kept poor, and only the Lords of the Land grow rich. When we black folk are alone together, we point to the poor whites and croon with vindictiveness:

I don't like liver
I don't like hash
I'd rather be a nigger
Than poor white trash....

And then, conversely, when we compare our hopelessness with the vast vistas of progress about us, when we feel self-disgust at our bare lot, when we contemplate our lack of courage in the face of daily force, we are seized with a desire to escape our shameful identification; and, overwhelmed emotionally, we seek to become protectively merged with the least-known and farthest removed race of men we know; yes, when we weigh ourselves and find ourselves wanting, we say with a snicker of self-depreciation:

> *White folks is evil*
> *And niggers is too*
> *So glad I'm a Chinaman*
> *I don't know what to do....*

There is something "funny" about the hate of the poor whites for us and our hate for them. Our minds fight against it, but external reality freezes us into stances of mutual resistance. And the irony of it is that both of us, the poor white and the poor black, are spoken of by the Lords of the Land as "our men." When they stride along and see us working their fields, they point to us and speak of us as though they owned us, saying: "There are our men." Jobs are few and the Lords of the Land know it, and when they refer to us, black or white, we are always "somebody's men."

So we stay fixed in attitudes of opposition, as though the Lords of the Land had waved a magic wand and cast a spell upon us, a spell from which we cannot awaken. And we blacks and whites ride down the years as the plantation system gnaws at the foundations of our characters. The plantation warps us so that some say we black and white upon the land cannot learn to live as other men do. But we know otherwise; we can learn. The Lords of the Land stand in our way; they do not permit the poor whites to make common union with us, for that would mean the end of the Lords' power. To ask questions, to protest, to insist, to contend for a secure institutional and political base upon which to stand and fulfill ourselves is equivalent to a new and intensified declaration of war.

Sometimes a few of us escape the sharecropping system and become home-owners. But gray and blue eyes watch us and if we do not help them in their game of "keeping the niggers down," if we do not ally ourselves with them and partake of their attitudes toward our own black folk, they find fault with us and drive us from our homes. An independent and prosperous black family flourishing amid a vast area of poverty is in itself a powerful enough symbol of aspiration to be a source of trouble, for that black family's mere well-being prods the black thousands, who, if they moved, would disrupt the delicately balanced forces of racial and economic power in the South.

But in spite of this, how eagerly have we taken to the culture of this new land when opportunity was open to us! Knowing no culture but this, what can we do but live in terms of what we see before our eyes each day? From the simple physiological reactions of slave days, from casual relations and sporadic hope, we learn to live the way of life of the Western world. Behind our pushing is the force of life itself, as strong in black men as in white, as emergent in us as in those who contrive to keep us down.

We hear men talk vaguely of a government in far-away Washington, a government that stands above the people and desires the welfare of all. We do not know this government; but the men it hires to execute its laws are the Lords of the Land whom we have known all our lives. We hear that the government wants to help us, but we are too far down at the bottom of the ditch for the fingers of the government to reach us, and there are too many men—the Lords of the Land and the poor whites—with their shoulders pressing tightly together in racial solidarity, forming a wall between us and the government. More to keep faith alive in our hearts than from any conviction that our lot will be bettered, we cling to our hope that the government would help us if it could. But for three hundred years we have been forced to accept the word of men instead of written contracts, for three hundred years we have been forced to rely upon the whimsical kindness of others rather than upon legal agreements; and all this has grown into hallowed tradition, congealed into reflex habit, hardened into a daily ritual, backed by rope and fagot.

When you, your father, and your father's father have lived under a system that permits others to organize your life, how can you get a check the government sends you? The Lords of the Land receive your mail and when you go to the Big House to ask for your check, they look at you and say: "Boy, get back in the field and keep working. We'll take care of your check. Here, you'd better make your mark on it so's we can cash it. We'll feed you until it is used up." Ordinarily you are so deep in debt when you receive a check from the government that you sign it entirely over to the Lords of the Land and forget about it.

Our days are walled with cotton; we move casually among the whites and they move casually among us; our speech is drawled out with slow smiles; there are no loud arguments; no voices are raised in contention; no shouts of passion betray the desire of one to convince the other. It is impossible to debate or maneuver for advantage without colliding; then blood is spilt. Trapped by the plantation system, we beg bread of the Lords of the Land and they give it to us; they need us to work for them. Although our association partakes of an odd sort of father-child relationship, it is devoid of that affinity of blood that restrains the impulse to cruelty, empty of that sense of intimate understanding born of a long proximity of human lives.

We plow, plant, chop, and pick the cotton, working always toward a dark, mercurial goal. We hear that silk is becoming popular, that jute is taking the place of cotton in many lands, that factories are making clothing out of rayon, that scientists have invented a substance called nylon. All these are blows to the reign of Queen Cotton, and when she dies we do not know how many of us will die with her. Adding to our confusion is the gradual appearance of machines that can pick more cotton in one day than any ten of us. How can we win this race with death when our thin blood is set against the potency of gasoline, when our weak flesh is pitted against the strength of steel, when our loose muscles must vie with the power of tractors?

Our lives are walled with cotton

We plow and plant cotton

We chop cotton

We pick cotton

When Queen Cotton dies . . .

. . . how many of us will die with her?

Through the years rumor filters down to us of cotton being grown in Egypt, Russia, Japan, India, in lands whose names we cannot pronounce. We black folk are needed no longer to grow cotton to clothe the world. Moreover, we cannot imagine that there will be so many factories erected in the South—since there are thousands already manufacturing more goods than can be bought—that those of us who cannot earn our bread by growing cotton will get jobs in them. Our future on the plantation is a worry.

Of a summer night, sitting on our front porches, we discuss how "funny" it is that we who raise cotton to clothe the nation do not have handkerchiefs to wipe the sweat from our brows, do not have mattresses to sleep on; we need shirts, dresses, sheets, drawers, tablecloths. When our cotton returns to us—after having been spun and woven and dyed and wrapped in cellophane—its cost is beyond our reach. The Bosses of the Buildings, owners of the factories that turn out the mass of commodities we yearn to buy, have decided that no cheap foreign articles can come freely into the country to undersell the products made by "their own workers."

The years glide on and strange things come. The Lords of the Land, as the cotton market shrinks and prices fall, grow poor and become riding bosses, and the riding bosses grow poor and become tenant farmers, and the tenant farmers grow poor and become sharecroppers, and the sharecroppers grow poor and become day laborers, migrants upon the land whose home is where the next crop is. We ask how such things can happen and we are told that the South is "broke," that it has to borrow money from the Bosses of the Buildings, that it must pay dearly for this hired gold, and that the soil is yielding less because of erosion. As plantation after plantation fails, the Bosses of the Buildings acquire control and send tractors upon the land, and still more of us are compelled to search for "another place." The Bosses of the Buildings now own almost one-third of the plantations of the South, and they are rapidly converting them into "farm factories."

When we grumble about our hard life, the Lords of the Land cry:

"Listen, I've borrowed money on my plantation and I'm risking my *land* with you folks!" And we, hungry and barefoot, cry: "And we're risking our *lives* with you!" And that is all that can be said; there is no room for idle words. Everything fits flush, each corner fitting tight into another corner. If you act at all, it is either to flee or to kill; you are either a victim or a rebel.

Days come and days go, but our lives upon the land remain without hope. We do not care if the barns rot down; they do not belong to us, anyway. No matter what improvement we may make upon the plantation, it would give us no claim upon the crop. In cold weather we burn everything in sight to keep us warm; we strip boards from our shacks and palings from the straggling fences. During long winter days we sit in cabins that have no windowpanes; the floors and roofs are made of thin planks of pine.

Out in the backyard, over a hole dug in the clay, stands a horizontal slab of oak with an oval opening in it; when it rains, a slow stink drifts over the wet fields.

To supplement our scanty rations, we take our buckets and roam the hillsides for berries, nuts, or wild greens; sometimes we fish in the creeks; at other times our black women tramp the fields looking for bits of fire-wood, piling their aprons high, coming back to our cabins slowly, like laden donkeys.

If our shacks catch fire, there is nothing much we can do but to snatch our children and run to a safe place and watch the flames eat the dry timbers. There is no fire wagon and there is but little water. Fire, like other things, has its way with us.

Lord, we *know* that this is a hard system! Even while we are hating the Lords of the Land, we know that if they paid us a just wage for all the work we do in raising a bale of cotton, the fleecy strands would be worth more than their weight in gold! Cotton is a drug, and for three hundred years we have taken it to kill the pain of hunger; but it does not ease our suffering. Most people take morphine out of choice; we take cotton because we must. For years longer than we remember, cotton has been our companion; we travel down the plantation road with debt holding our left hand, with credit holding our right, and ahead of us looms the grave, the final and simple end.

We move slowly through sun and rain, and our eyes grow dull and our skin sags. For hours we sit on our porches and stare out over the dusty land, wondering why we are so tired. In the fall the medicine men come and set up their tents, light gas flares, and amuse us with crude jokes. We take the pennies out of the tin can under a plank in the barn and buy patent medicine for Grandpa's malaria-like feeling, for Grandma's sudden chills, for Susie's spasms of hotness, for the strange and nasty rash that eats at Rosa's skin, for Bob's hacking cough that will not leave, for the pain that gnaws the baby's stomach day and night.

Yet we live on and our families grow large. Some people wag their heads in amusement when they see our long lines of ragged children, but we love them. If our families are large, we have a chance to make a bigger crop, for there are more hands to tend the land. But large families eat more, and, although our children lighten the burden of toil, we finish the year as we were before, hungry and in debt. Like black buttercups, our children spring up on the red soil of the plantations. When a new one arrives, neighbors from miles around come and look at it, speculating upon which parent it resembles. A child is a glad thing in the bleak stretches of the cotton country, and our gold is in the hearts of the people we love, in the veins that carry our blood, upon those faces where we catch furtive glimpses of the shape of our humble souls.

Our way of life is simple and our unit of living is formed by the willingness of two or more of us to organize ourselves voluntarily to make a crop, to pool our labor power to wrest subsistence from the stubborn soil. We live just as man lived when he first struggled against this earth. After having been pulverized by slavery and purged of our cultural heritage, we have been kept so far from the sentiments and ideals of the Lords of the Land that we do not feel their way of life deeply enough to act upon their assumptions and motives. So, living by folk tradition, possessing but a few rights which others respect, we are unable to establish our family groups upon a basis of property ownership. For the most part our delicate families are held together by love, sympathy, pity, and the goading knowledge that we must work together to make a crop.

That is why we black folk laugh and sing when we are alone together. There is nothing—no ownership or lust for power—that stands between us and our kin. And we reckon kin not as others do, but down to the ninth and tenth cousin. And for a reason we cannot explain we are mighty proud when we meet a man, woman, or child who, in talking to us, reveals that the blood of our brood has somehow entered his veins. Because our eyes are not blinded by the hunger for possessions, we are a tolerant folk. A black mother who stands in the sagging door of her gingerbread shack may weep as she sees her children straying off into the unknown world, but no matter what they may do, no matter what happens to them, no matter what crimes they may commit, no matter what the world may think of them, that mother always welcomes them back with an irreducibly human feeling that stands above the claims of law or property. Our scale of values differs from that of the world from which we have been excluded; our shame is not its shame, and our love is not its love.

Our black children are born to us in our one-room shacks, before crackling log fires, with rusty scissors boiling in tin pans, with black plantation midwives hovering near, with pine-knot flames casting shadows upon the wooden walls, with the sound of kettles of water singing over the fires in the hearths. . . .

As our children grow up they help us day by day, fetching pails of water from the springs, gathering wood for cooking, sweeping the floors, minding the younger children, stirring the clothes boiling in black pots over the fires in the backyards, and making butter in the churns. . . .

Sometimes there is a weather-worn, pine-built schoolhouse for our children, but even if the school were open for the full term our children would not have the time to go. We cannot let them leave the fields when cotton is waiting to be picked. When the time comes to break the sod, the sod must be broken; when the time comes to plant the seeds, the seeds must be planted; and when the time comes to loosen the red clay from about the bright green stalks of the cotton plants, that, too, must be done even if it is September and school is open. Hunger is the punishment if we violate the laws of Queen Cotton. The seasons of the year form the mold that shapes our lives, and who can change the seasons?

Deep down we distrust the schools that the Lords of the Land build for us and we do not really feel that they are ours. In many states they edit the textbooks that our children study, for the most part deleting all references to government, voting, citizenship, and civil rights. Many of them say that French, Latin, and Spanish are languages not for us, and they become angry when they think that we desire to learn more than they want us to. They say that "all the geography a nigger needs to know is how to get from his shack to the plow." They restrict our education easily, inasmuch as their laws decree that there must be schools for our black children and schools for the white, churches for our black folk and churches for the white, and in public places their signs read: FOR COLORED and FOR WHITE. They have arranged the order of life in the South so that a different set of ideals is inculcated in the opposing black and white groups.

Yet, in a vague, sentimental sort of way we love books inordinately, even though we do not know how to read them, for we know that books are the gateway to a forbidden world. Any black man who can read a book is a hero to us. And we are joyful when we hear a black man speak like a book. The people who say how the world is to be run, who have fires in winter, who wear warm clothes, who get enough to eat, are the people who make books speak to them. Sometimes of a night we tell our children

to get out the old big family Bible and read to us, and we listen wonderingly until, tired from a long day in the fields, we fall asleep.

The Lords of the Land have shown us how preciously they regard books by the manner in which they cheat us in erecting schools for our children. They tax black and white equally throughout the state, and then they divide the money for education unequally, keeping most of it for their own schools, generally taking five dollars for themselves for every dollar they give us. For example, in the state of Mississippi, for every $25 a year that is spent to educate a white child, only $5 a year is spent to educate a black child. In many counties there is no school at all, and where there is one, it is old, with a leaky roof; our children sit on wooden planks made into crude benches without backs. Sometimes seventy children, ranging in age from six to twenty, crowd into the one room which comprises the entire school structure; they are taught by one teacher whose wage is lower and whose conditions of work are immeasurably poorer than those of white teachers.

sustained act of knowledge + information of memory

Many of our schools are open for only six months a year, and allow our children to progress only to the sixth grade. Some of those who are lucky enough to graduate go back as teachers to instruct their brothers and sisters. Many of our children grow to feel that they would rather remain upon the plantations to work than attend school, for they can observe so few tangible results in the lives of those who do attend.

The schoolhouse is usually far away; at times our children must travel distances varying from one to six miles. Busses are furnished for many white children, but rarely for ours. The distances we walk are so legendary that often the measure of a black man's desire to obtain an education is gauged by the number of miles he declares he walked to school when a child.

Sunday is always a glad day. We call all our children to us and comb the hair of the boys and plait the hair of the girls; then we rub their heads with hog fat to make their hair shine. We wrap the girls' hair in white strings and put a red ribbon upon their heads; we make the boys wear stocking caps, that is, we make them pull upon their heads the tops of our stockings, cut and stretched taut upon their skulls to keep their hair in place. Then we rub the hog fat upon their faces to take that dull, ashy look away from skins made dry and rough from the weather of the fields. In clean clothes ironed stiff with starch made from flour, we hitch up the mule to the wagon, pile in our Bibles and baskets of food—hog meat and greens —and we are off to church.

The preacher tells of days long ago and of a people whose sufferings were like ours. He preaches of the Hebrew children and the fiery furnace, of Daniel, of Moses, of Solomon, and of Christ. What we have not dared feel in the presence of the Lords of the Land, we now feel in church. Our hearts and bodies, reciprocally acting upon each other, swing out into the meaning of the story the preacher is unfolding. Our eyes become absorbed in a vision. . . .

. . . a place eternal filled with happiness where dwell God and His many hosts of angels singing His praises and glorifying His name and in the midst of this oneness of being there arises one whose soul is athirst to feel things for himself and break away from the holy band of joy and he organizes revolt in Heaven and preaches rebellion and aspires to take the place of God to rule Eternity and God condemns him from Heaven and decrees that he shall be banished and this Rebel this Satan this Lucifer persuades one-third of all the many hosts of angels in Heaven to follow him

and build a new Heaven and down he comes with his angels whose hearts are black with pride and whose souls are hot with vengeance against God who decides to make Man and He makes Man in His own image and He forms him of clay and He breathes the breath of life into him but He warns him against the Rebel the Satan the Lucifer who had been banished from Heaven for his pride and envy and Man lives in a garden of peace where there is no Time no Sorrow and no Death and while Man lives in this *happiness there comes to him the Rebel the Satan the Lucifer and he tempts Man and drags him down the same black path of rebellion and sin and God seeing this decrees that Man shall live in the Law and not Love and must endure Toil and Pain and Death and must dig for his bread in the stony earth but while Man suffers God's compassion is moved and God Himself assumes the form of Man's corrupt and weak flesh and comes down and lives and suffers and dies upon a cross to show Man the way back*

up the broad highway to peace and thus Man begins to live for a time under a new dispensation of Love and not Law and the Rebel the Satan the Lucifer still works rebellion seducing persuading falsifying and God through His prophets says that He will come for a second time bringing not peace but a sword to rout the powers of darkness and build a new Jerusalem and God through His prophets says that the final fight the last battle the Armageddon will be resumed and will endure until the end of Time and of Death. . . .

. . . and the preacher's voice is sweet to us, caressing and lashing, conveying to us a heightening of consciousness that the Lords of the Land would rather keep from us, filling us with a sense of hope that is treasonable to the rule of Queen Cotton. As the sermon progresses, the preacher's voice increases in emotional intensity, and we, in tune and sympathy with his sweeping story, sway in our seats until we have lost all notion of time and have begun to float on a tide of passion. The preacher begins to punctuate his words with sharp rhythms, and we are lifted far beyond the boundaries of our daily lives, upward and outward, until, drunk with our enchanted vision, our senses lifted to the burning skies, we do not know who we are, what we are, or where we are. . . .

We go home pleasantly tired and sleep easily, for we know that we hold somewhere within our hearts a possibility of inexhaustible happiness; we know that if we could but get our feet planted firmly upon this earth, we could laugh and live and build. We take this feeling with us each day and it drains the gall out of our years, sucks the sting from the rush of time, purges the pain from our memory of the past, and banishes the fear of loneliness and death. When the soil grows poorer, we cling to this feeling; when clanking tractors uproot and hurl us from the land, we cling to it; when our eyes behold a black body swinging from a tree in the wind, we cling to it. . . .

Some say that, because we possess this faculty of keeping alive this spark of happiness under adversity, we are children. No, it is the courage and faith in simple living that enable us to maintain this reservoir of human feeling, for we know that there will come a day when we shall pour out our hearts over this land.

Neither are we ashamed to go of a Saturday night to the crossroad dancehall and slow drag, ball the jack, and Charleston to an old guitar and piano. Dressed in starched jeans, an old silk shirt, a big straw hat, we swing the girls over the plank floor, clapping our hands, stomping our feet, and singing:

Shake it to the east
Shake it to the west
Shake it to the one
You love the best. . . .

It is what makes our boys and girls, when they are ten or twelve years of age, roam the woods, bareheaded and barefoot, singing and whistling and shouting in wild, hilarious chorus a string of ditties that make the leaves of the trees shiver in naked and raucous laughter.

> *I love you once*
> *I love you twice*
> *I love you next to*
> *Jesus Christ....*

And it is this same capacity for joy that makes us hymn:

> *I'm a stranger*
> *Don't drive me away*
> *I'm a stranger*
> *Don't drive me away*
> *If you drive me away*
> *You may need me some day*
> *I'm a stranger*
> *Don't drive me away....*

But there are times when we doubt our songs; they are not enough to unify our fragile folk lives in this competitive world. As our children grow older, they leave us to fulfill the sense of happiness that sleeps in their hearts. Unlike us, they have been influenced by the movies, magazines, and glimpses of town life, and they lack the patience to wait for the consummation of God's promise as we do. We despair to see them go, but we tell them that we want them to escape the deadening life of the plantation. Our hearts are divided: we want them to have a new life, yet we are afraid if they challenge the Lords of the Land, for we know that terror will assail them. As our children learn what is happening on other plantations and up north, the casual ties of our folk families begin to dissolve.

There are times . . .

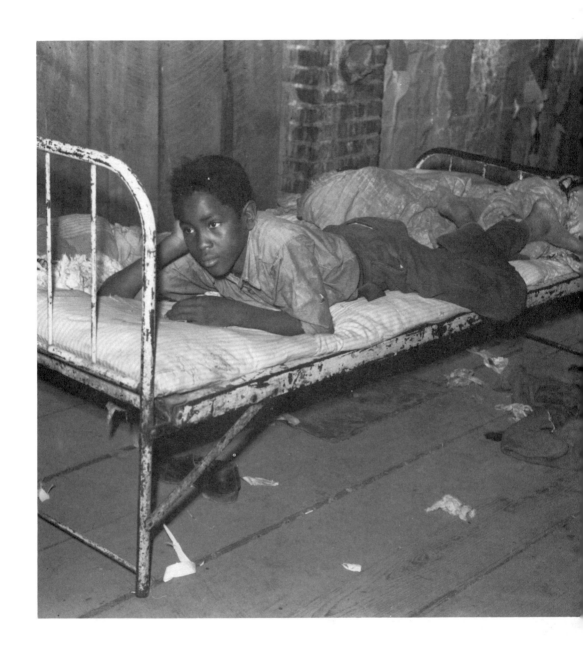

. . . when we doubt our songs

Vast changes engulf our lives. We sit on our front porches, fanning the flies away, and watch the men with axes come through the Southland, as they have already gone through the Northland and the Westland, and whack down the pine, oak, ash, elm, and hickory trees, leaving the land denuded as far as the eye can see. And then rain comes in leaden sheets to slant and scour at the earth until it washes away rich layers of top soil, until it leaves the land defenseless, until all vegetation is gone and nothing remains to absorb the moisture and hinder the violent spreading floods of early spring.

Cotton crops have sapped the soil of its fertility; twenty or thirty years of good cotton farming are enough to drain the land and leave it a hard, yellow mat, a mockery to the sky and a curse to us.

On top of this there come, with a tread as of doom, more and more of the thundering tractors and cotton-picking machines that more and more render our labor useless. Year by year these machines grow from one odd and curious object to be gaped at to thousands that become so deadly in their impersonal labor that we grow to hate them. They do our work better and faster than we can, driving us from plantation to plantation. Black and white alike now go to the pea, celery, orange, grapefruit, cabbage, and lemon crops. Sometimes we walk and sometimes the bosses of the farm factories send their trucks for us. We go from the red land to the brown land, from the brown land to the black land, working our way eastward until we reach the blue Atlantic. In spring we chop cotton in Mississippi and pick beans in Florida; in summer we labor in the peach orchards of Georgia and tramp on to the tobacco crop in North Carolina; then we trek to New Jersey to dig potatoes. We sleep in woods, in barns, in wooden barracks, on sidewalks, and sometimes in jail. Our dog-trot, dog-run, shot-gun, and gingerbread shacks fill with ghosts and tumble down from rot.

The bosses send their trucks for us

We labor in the farm factories

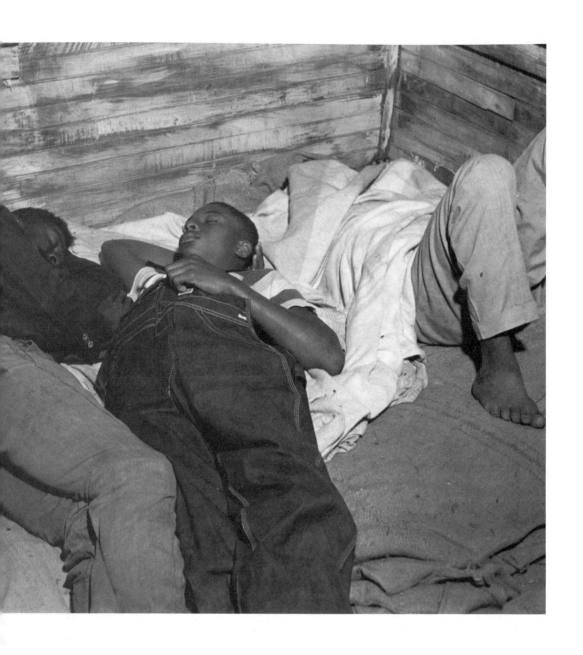

We sleep . . .

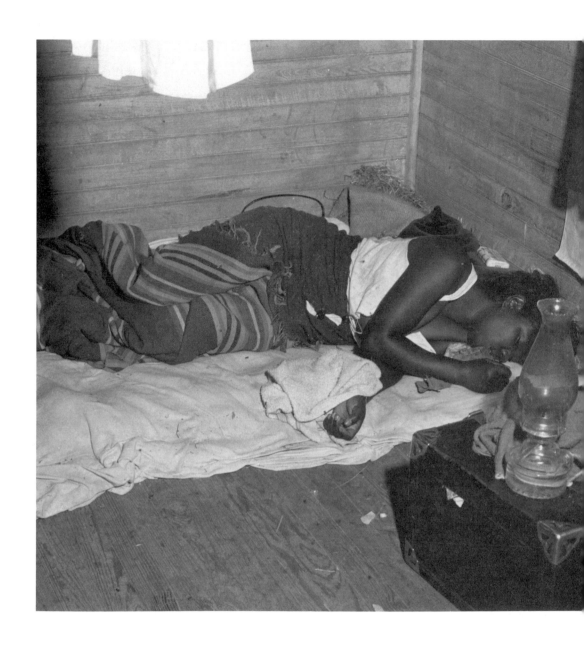

. . . in wooden barracks

News comes that there are better places to go, but we know that the next place will be as bad as the last one. Yet we go. Our drifting is the expression of our hope to improve our lives. Season after season the farm factories pass before our eyes, and at the end of the long journey we are filled with nostalgic melancholy, a blurred picture of many places seen and suffered in, a restlessness which we cannot appease.

In 1914, out of the unknown, comes the news that a war is in progress to hold back the Germans, who are determined to wrest markets and lands away from other countries. We hear that the government has decided to keep alien labor out of the country, and a call is made to us to come north and help turn the wheels of industry. At the thought of leaving our homes again, we cry: "What a life it is we live! Our roots are nowhere! We have no home even upon this soil which formed our blood and bones!" But hundreds of thousands of us get on the move once more.

The Lords of the Land pause now and speak kind words to us; they want us to remain upon the plantations. They tell us that they are our best friends; we smile and say nothing. As we abandon the land, odd things happen to us. If one of us should run afoul of the law at harvest time, the Lords of the Land will speak a good word to the sheriff for "his niggers." The law listens and turns us over to the Lords of the Land who pay our fines. Then we labor upon the plantation to pay the debt! But as long as we merely drift from plantation to plantation, the Lords of the Land do not really care. They say: "Niggers don't know what they want. Niggers come and niggers go, but we'll always have the niggers. Only it's hard to keep the books with them moving all the time."

Soon, however, they take a more serious attitude toward us, for the Bosses of the Buildings send men with fair words down from the North, telling us how much money we can make digging in the mines, smelting ore, laying rails, and killing hogs. They tell us that we will live in brick buildings, that we will vote, that we will be able to send our children to school for nine months of the year, that if we get into trouble we will not be lynched, and that we will not have to grin, doff our hats, bend our knees, slap our thighs, dance, and laugh when we see a white face. We listen, and it sounds like religion. Is it really true? Is there not a trick somewhere? We have grown to distrust all white men. Yet they say: "Listen, we need you to work. We'll hire trains to take you away." Then the weekly Negro newspapers supplement their pleas; the Chicago *Defender,* the Pittsburgh *Courier,* the Baltimore *Afro-American,* and many other newspapers paint the North as a land of promise. We cannot help but believe now. We cannot work the cotton fields for thinking of it; our minds are paralyzed with the hope and dread of it. Not to go means lingering here to live out this slow death; to go means facing the unknown. But, strangely, life has already prepared us for moving and drifting. Have we not already roamed the South? Yes, we will go and see. But we do not move. We are scared. Who will go first? Then, suddenly, a friend leaves and we whisper to him to write and tell us if the dream is true. We wait. Word comes. It *is* true! "Come on!" the letters tell us. We go.

It is like this: suddenly, while we are chopping at the clods of clay with a heavy hoe, the riding boss gallops up and says: "Hurry up there, nigger!"

Perhaps for the first time in our lives we straighten our backs, drop the hoe, give a fleeting glance at the white man's face, and walk off.

"Hey, where the hell you going, nigger?"

"I'm shaking the dust of the South off my feet, white man."

"You'll starve up north, nigger."

"I don't care. I'm going to die some day anyhow."

But so many of us are leaving that the Lords of the Land begin to worry.

"Don't go," they say.

"We're already going," we say, and keep leaving.

If we have no money, we borrow it; if we cannot borrow it, we beg it. If the Bosses of the Buildings do not furnish us with a train, we walk until we reach a railroad and then we swing onto a freight. There develops such a shortage of labor in the South that the Lords of the Land order us rounded up and threatened with jail sentences unless we consent to go to the fields and gather the waiting crops. Finally they persuade men of our own race to talk to us.

"Let down your buckets where you are," our black leaders say.

"We're leaving," we answer.

"The white man of the South is your friend," they say.

"How much are they paying you to say that?" we ask.

"You'll freeze up north."

"We don't care."

The Lords of the Land say: "You niggers are going north because you think you'll mix with whites."

"Look at all the half-white boys and girls on the plantations," we answer. "We black men did not do that."

"Don't talk fresh, nigger!"

"We ain't talking; we're leaving!"

"Come on; we'll build you a big school!"

"We'd rather be a lamppost in Chicago than the president of Dixie!"

While we are leaving, our black boys come back from Flanders, telling us of how their white officers of the United States Army had treated them, how they had kept them in labor battalions, how they had jim-crowed them in the trenches even when they were fighting and dying, how the white officers had instructed the French people to segregate them. Our boys come back to Dixie in uniform and walk the streets with quick steps and proud shoulders. They cannot help it; they have been in battle, have seen men of all nations and races die. They have seen what men are made of, and now they act differently. But the Lords of the Land cannot understand them. They take them and lynch them while they are still wearing the uniform of the United States Army.

Our black boys do not die for liberty in Flanders. They die in Texas and

Georgia. Atlanta is our Marne. Brownsville, Texas, is our Château-Thierry.

It is a lesson we will never forget; it is written into the pages of our blood, into the ledgers of our bleeding bodies, into columns of judgment figures and balance statements in the lobes of our brains.

"Don't do this!" we cry.

"Nigger, shut your damn mouth!" they say.

"Don't lynch us!" we plead.

"You're not white!" they say.

"Why don't somebody say something?" we ask.

"We told you to shut your damn mouth!"

We listen for somebody to say something, and we still travel, leaving the South. Our eyes are open, our ears listening for words to point the way.

From 1890 to 1920, more than 2,000,000 of us left the land.

3.

Death on the City Pavements

LORD IN HEAVEN! Good God Almighty! Great Day in the Morning! It's here! Our time has come! We are leaving! We are angry no more; we are leaving! We are bitter no more; we are leaving! We are leaving our homes, pulling up stakes to move on. We look up at the high southern sky and remember all the sunshine and the rain and we feel a sense of loss, but we are leaving. We look out at the wide green fields which our eyes saw when we first came into the world and we feel full of regret, but we are leaving. We scan the kind black faces we have looked upon since we first saw the light of day, and, though pain is in our hearts, we are leaving. We take one last furtive look over our shoulders to the Big House—high upon a hill beyond the railroad tracks—where the Lord of the Land lives, and we feel glad, for we are leaving. . . .

For a long time now we have heard tell that all over the world men are leaving the land for the streets of the city, so we are leaving too. As we leave we see thousands of the poor whites also packing up to move to the city, leaving the land that will not give life to her sons and daughters, black or white. When a man lives upon the land and is cold and hungry and hears word of the great factories going up in the cities, he begins to hope and dream of a new life, and he leaves.

In 1890 there were 1,500,000 of us black men and women in the cities of the nation, both north and south. In 1900 there were 2,000,000 of us. In 1920 there were 3,500,000 of us in the cities of the nation and we were still going, still leaving the land. So many of us crowded into New York City that Harlem's black population doubled between 1900 and 1920. In Philadelphia our influx increased the number of black people by one-third in a few years. In Chicago our endless trek inflated the Black Belt population by more than 125,000 from 1920 to 1930. And our tide continued to roll from the farm to the factory, from the country to the city.

Perhaps never in history has a more utterly unprepared folk wanted to go to the city; we were barely born as a folk when we headed for the tall and sprawling centers of steel and stone. We, who were landless upon the land; we, who had barely managed to live in family groups; we, who needed the ritual and guidance of institutions to hold our atomized lives together in lines of purpose; we, who had known only relationships to people and not relationships to things; we who had never belonged to any organizations except the church and burial societies; we, who had had our personalities blasted with two hundred years of slavery and had been turned loose to shift for ourselves—we were such a folk as this when we moved into a world that was destined to test all we were, that threw us into the scales of competition to weigh our mettle. And how were we to know that, the moment we landless millions of the land—we men who were struggling to be born—set our awkward feet upon the pavements of the city, life would begin to exact of us a heavy toll in death?

**We, who had barely managed
to live in family groups**

We, who needed the ritual and
guidance of institutions

We, who had never belonged to any organizations
except the church and burial societies

We, who had had our personalities blasted with
two hundred years of slavery

We did not know what would happen, what was in store for us. We went innocently, longing and hoping for a life that the Lords of the Land would not let us live. Our hearts were high as we moved northward to the cities. What emotions, fears, what a complex of sensations we felt when, looking out of a train window at the revolving fields, we first glimpsed the sliding waters of the gleaming Ohio! What memories that river evoked in us, memories black and gloomy, yet tinged with the bright border of a wild and desperate hope! The Ohio is more than a river. It is a symbol, a line that runs through our hearts, dividing hope from despair, just as once it bisected the nation, dividing freedom from slavery. How many desperate scenes have been enacted upon its banks! How many grim dramas have been played out upon its bosom! How many slave hunters and Abolitionists have clashed here with fire in their eyes and deep convictions in their hearts! This river has seen men whose beliefs were so strong that the rights of property meant nothing, men whose feelings were so mighty that the laws of the land meant nothing, men whose passions were so fiery that only human life and human dignity mattered.

The train and the auto move north, ever north, and from 1916 to 1928, 1,200,000 of us were moving from the South to the North and we kept leaving. Night and day, in rain and in sun, in winter and in summer, we leave the land. Already, as we sit and look broodingly out over the turning fields, we notice with attention and hope that the dense southern swamps give way to broad, cultivated wheat farms. The spick-and-span farmhouses done in red and green and white crowd out the casual, unpainted ginger-bread shacks. Silos take the place of straggling piles of hay. Macadam highways now wind over the horizon instead of dirt roads. The cheeks of the farm people are full and ruddy, not sunken and withered like soda crackers. The slow southern drawl, which in legend is so sweet and hos-pitable but which in fact has brought down on our black bodies suffering untold, is superseded by clipped Yankee phrases, phrases spoken with such rapidity and neutrality that we, with our slow ears, have difficulty in understanding. And the foreigners—Poles, Germans, Swedes, and Italians—we never dreamed that there were so many in the world! Yes, coming north for a Negro sharecropper involves more strangeness than going to another country. It is the beginning of living on a new and terrifying plane of consciousness.

We see white men and women get on the train, dressed in expensive new clothes. We look at them guardedly and wonder will they bother us. Will they ask us to stand up while they sit down? Will they tell us to go to the back of the coach? Even though we have been told that we need not be afraid, we have lived so long in fear of all white faces that we cannot help but sit and wait. We look around the train and we do not see the old familiar signs: FOR COLORED and FOR WHITE. The train speeds north and we cannot sleep. Our heads sink in a doze, and then we sit bolt-upright, prodded by the thought that we must watch these strange surroundings. But nothing happens; these white men seem impersonal and their very neutrality reassures us—for a while. Almost against our deeper judgment, we try to force ourselves to relax, for these brisk men give no sign of what they feel. They are indifferent. O sweet and welcome *indifference!*

The miles click behind us. Into Chicago, Indianapolis, New York, Cleveland, Buffalo, Detroit, Toledo, Philadelphia, Pittsburgh, and Milwaukee we go, looking for work. We feel freer than we have ever felt before, but we are still a little scared. It is like a dream. Will we wake up suddenly and find that none of this is really true, that we are merely daydreaming behind the barn, snoozing in the sun, waiting to hear the hoarse voice of the riding boss saying: "Nigger, where do you think you are? Get the hell up from there and move on!"

Timidly, we get off the train. We hug our suitcases, fearful of pickpockets, looking with unrestrained curiosity at the great big brick buildings. We are very reserved, for we have been warned not to act "green," that the city people can spot a "sucker" a mile away. Then we board our first Yankee street car to go to a cousin's home, a brother's home, a sister's home, a friend's home, an uncle's home, or an aunt's home. We pay the conductor our fare and look about apprehensively for a seat. We have been told that we can sit where we please, but we are still scared. We cannot shake off three hundred years of fear in three hours. We ease into a seat and look out of the window at the crowded streets. A white man or a white woman comes and sits beside us, not even looking at us, as though this were a normal thing to do. The muscles of our bodies tighten. Indefinable sensations crawl over our skins and our blood tingles. Out of the corners of our eyes we try to get a glimpse of the strange white face that floats but a few inches from ours. The impulses to laugh and to cry clash in us; we bite our lips and stare out of the window.

There are so many people. For the first time in our lives we feel human bodies, strangers whose lives and thoughts are unknown to us, pressing always close about us. We cannot see or know a *man* because of the thousands upon thousands of *men*. The apartments in which we sleep are crowded and noisy, and soon enough we learn that the brisk, clipped men of the North, the Bosses of the Buildings, are not at all *indifferent*. They are deeply concerned about us, but in a new way. It seems as though we are now living inside of a machine; days and events move with a hard reasoning of their own. We live amid swarms of people, yet there is a vast distance between people, a distance that words cannot bridge. No longer do our lives depend upon the soil, the sun, the rain, or the wind; we live by the grace of jobs and the brutal logic of jobs. We do not know this world, or what makes it move. In the South life was different; men spoke to you, cursed you, yelled at you, or killed you. The world moved by signs we knew. But here in the North cold forces hit you and push you. It is a world of *things*.

Our defenseless eyes cloud with bewilderment when we learn that there are not enough houses for us to live in. And competing with us for shelter are thousands of poor migrant whites who have come up from the South, just as we have come. The cost of building a house is high, and building activities are on the downgrade. It is wartime; no new labor is coming in from the old countries across the seas. The only district we can live in is the area just beyond the business belt, a transition area where a sooty conglomeration of factories and mills belches smoke that stains our clothes and lungs.

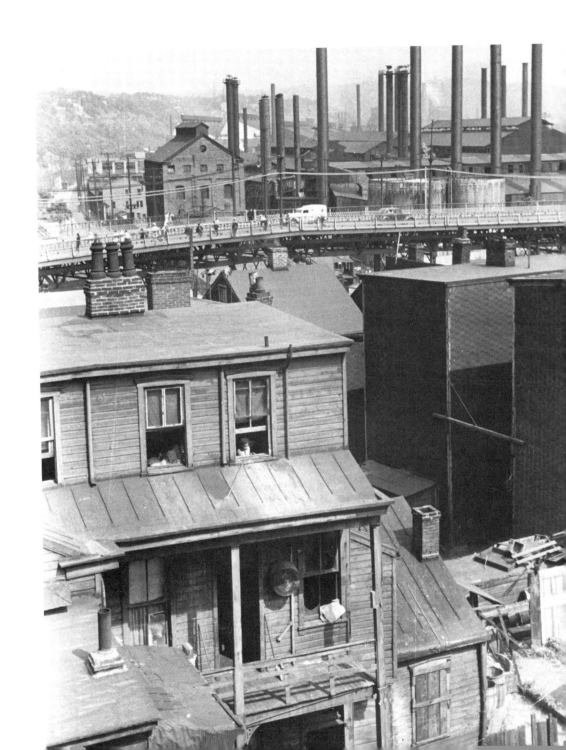

We black folk are not the only ones who move into this so-called transition area; it is the first port of call for that incoming horde of men who float continuously into cities. The tenements we live in are old; they are rarely repaired or replaced. On most of our buildings are signs: THIS PROPERTY IS FOR SALE. Any day we can be told to move, that our home is to be torn down to make way for a new factory or a new mill.

So, under the black mourning pall of smoke from the stacks of American industry, our observing Negro eyes watch a thousand rivulets of blood melt, fuse, blend, and flow in a common stream of human unity as it merges with the great American tide. But we never mix with that stream; we are not allowed to. For years we watch the timid faces of poor white peasants—Turks, Czechs, Croats, Finns, and Greeks—pass through this curtain of smoke and emerge with the sensitive features of modern men. But our faces do not change. Our cheek-bones remain as unaltered as the stony countenance of the Sphinx.

From this transition area we watch many of the immigrants move on to the rooming-house district which almost always borders the transition area of the big industrial city; later many of them move from the rooming-house area into the apartment-house district. After that the only news we hear of some of them is what we read in the newspapers. Of a morning, years later, we pick up the Chicago *Daily Tribune,* or the Cleveland *Plain Dealer,* or the Detroit *Free Press,* or the Philadelphia *Inquirer,* or the New York *Times,* and see that some former neighbors of ours, a Mr. and Mrs. Klein or Murphy or Potaci or Pierre or Cromwell or Stepanovich and their children—kids we once played with upon the slag piles—are now living in the suburban areas, having swum upstream through the American waters of opportunity into the professional classes.

Times without number our eyes witness this drama. The gigantic American companies will not employ our daughters in their offices as clerks, bookkeepers, or stenographers; huge department stores will not employ our young women, fresh from school, as saleswomen. The engineering, aviation, mechanical, and chemical schools close their doors to our sons, just as the great corporations which make thousands of commodities refuse to employ them. The Bosses of the Buildings decree that we must be maids, porters, janitors, cooks, and general servants.

We remain to live in the clinging soot just beyond the factory areas, behind the railroad tracks, near the river banks, under the viaducts, by the steel and iron mills, on the edges of the coal and lumber yards. We live in crowded, barn-like rooms, in old rotting buildings where once dwelt rich native whites of a century ago. Because we are black, because our love of life gives us many children, because we do not have quiet ways of doing things, because the outdoor boisterousness of the plantation still clings to us, because we move slowly and speak slowly, white people say that we are destructive and therefore do not want us in their neighborhoods. When we return home at night from our jobs, we are afraid to venture into other sections of the city, for we fear that the white boys will gang up and molest us. When we do go out into white neighborhoods, we always go in crowds, for that is the best mode of protection.

White people say that they are afraid of us, and it often makes us laugh. When they see one of us, they either smile with contempt or amusement. When they see *two* of us, they treat us as though some grave thought were on their minds. When they see *four* of us, they are usually silent. When they see *six* of us, they become downright apprehensive and alarmed. And because they are afraid of us, we are afraid of them. Especially do we feel fear when we meet the gangs of white boys who have been taught—at home and at school—that we black folk are making their parents lose their homes and life's savings because we have moved into their neighborhoods.

They say our presence in their neighborhoods lowers the value of their property. We do not understand why this should be so. We are poor; but they were once poor, too. They make up their minds, because others tell them to, that they must move at once if we rent an apartment near them. Having been warned against us by the Bosses of the Buildings, having

heard tall tales about us, about how "bad" we are, they react emotionally as though we had the plague when we move into their neighborhoods. Is it any wonder, then, that their homes are suddenly and drastically reduced in value? They hastily abandon them, sacrificing them to the Bosses of the Buildings, the men who instigate all this for whatever profit they can get in real-estate sales. And in the end we are the "fall guys." When the white folks move, the Bosses of the Buildings let the property to us at rentals higher than those the whites paid.

And the Bosses of the Buildings take these old houses and convert them into "kitchenettes," and then rent them to us at rates so high that they make fabulous fortunes before the houses are too old for habitation. What they do is this: they take, say, a seven-room apartment, which rents for $50 a month to whites, and cut it up into seven small apartments, of one room each; they install one small gas stove and one small sink in each room. The Bosses of the Buildings rent these kitchenettes to us at the rate of, say, $6 a week. Hence, the same apartment for which white people—who can get jobs anywhere and who receive higher wages than we—pay $50 a month is rented to us for $42 a week! And because there are not enough houses for us to live in, because we have been used to sleeping several in a room on the plantations in the South, we rent these kitchenettes and are glad to get them. These kitchenettes are our havens from the plantations in the South. We have fled the wrath of Queen Cotton and we are tired.

Sometimes five or six of us live in a one-room kitchenette, a place where simple folk such as we should never be held captive. A war sets up in our emotions: one part of our feelings tells us that it is good to be in the city, that we have a chance at life here, that we need but turn a corner to become a stranger, that we no longer need bow and dodge at the sight of the Lords of the Land. Another part of our feelings tells us that, in terms of worry and strain, the cost of living in the kitchenettes is too high, that the city heaps too much responsibility upon us and gives too little security in return.

The kitchenette is the author of the glad tidings that new suckers are in town, ready to be cheated, plundered, and put in their places.

The kitchenette is our prison, our death sentence without a trial, the new form of mob violence that assaults not only the lone individual, but all of us, in its ceaseless attacks.

The kitchenette, with its filth and foul air, with its one toilet for thirty or more tenants, kills our black babies so fast that in many cities twice as many of them die as white babies.

The kitchenette is the seed bed for scarlet fever, dysentery, typhoid, tuberculosis, gonorrhea, syphilis, pneumonia, and malnutrition.

The kitchenette scatters death so widely among us that our death rate exceeds our birth rate, and if it were not for the trains and autos bringing us daily into the city from the plantations, we black folks who dwell in northern cities would die out entirely over the course of a few years.

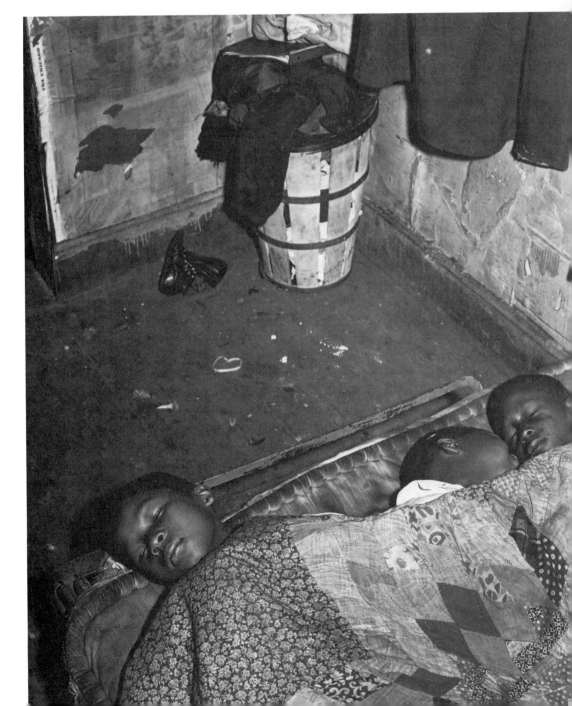

The kitchenette, with its crowded rooms and incessant bedlam, provides an enticing place for crimes of all sort—crimes against women and children or any stranger who happens to stray into its dark hallways. The noise of our living, boxed in stone and steel, is so loud that even a pistol shot is smothered.

The kitchenette throws desperate and unhappy people into an unbearable closeness of association, thereby increasing latent friction, giving birth to never-ending quarrels of recrimination, accusation, and vindictiveness, producing warped personalities.

The kitchenette injects pressure and tension into our individual personalities, making many of us give up the struggle, walk off and leave wives, husbands, and even children behind to shift as best they can.

The kitchenette creates thousands of one-room homes where our black mothers sit, deserted, with their children about their knees.

The kitchenette blights the personalities of our growing children, disorganizes them, blinds them to hope, creates problems whose effects can be traced in the characters of its child victims for years afterward.

The kitchenette jams our farm girls, while still in their teens, into rooms with men who are restless and stimulated by the noise and lights of the city; and more of our girls have bastard babies than the girls in any other sections of the city.

The kitchenette fills our black boys with longing and restlessness, urging them to run off from home, to join together with other restless black boys in gangs, that brutal form of city courage.

The kitchenette piles up mountains of profits for the Bosses of the Buildings and makes them ever more determined to keep things as they are.

The kitchenette reaches out with fingers full of golden bribes to the officials of the city, persuading them to allow old firetraps to remain standing and occupied long after they should have been torn down.

The kitchenette is the funnel through which our pulverized lives flow to ruin and death on the city pavements, at a profit. . . .

A few of our black boys save enough from their weekly wages to make payments on homes. But they discover that white home-owners refuse to sell to them and stand solid against any extension of the Black Belt. Meanwhile we continue to pour in from the South, swelling our numbers that live in these locked-in quarters. And then one day some shrewd white man, eager for a high profit, decides to sell his home to a black buyer, and for the first time a black family "invades" a white neighborhood and is greeted with violence. When our black fathers go to work in the mornings, they hear the muttered insults of their white neighbors. Bricks are hurled through the windows of our homes; garbage is tossed at our black children when they go to school; and finally bombs explode against our front doors. But whenever we can escape the terrors and limitations of the Black Belt, we move into the white area, disdainful of reprisal.

Grudgingly, the white population falls back, street by street, leaving its homes empty. Sometimes the members of a white family will board up their old homestead and move away, but not before they have cautioned their real-estate broker that no black folk should be allowed to purchase their property. The white families do not want black strangers to dwell within the walls of rooms made sacred to them through long years of intimate living.

With rows of empty houses at their disposal, the Bosses of the Buildings step in with the smiles of salesmanship. They purchase the abandoned properties, promising to respect the wishes of the owners, and then they immediately hang up placards, saying: NOW OPEN TO COLORED TENANTS. And we black folk, glad at long last to find living space, rush to sign leases at exorbitant rentals. In this manner we force the whites back year by year until the tide of our black life, pushing irresistibly outward, reaches the border of some restricted middle-class neighborhood, and then the warfare begins anew. Encouraged by powerful real-estate boards and business interests, home-owners hurriedly create property-owning associations to stem our black "invasion." If the situation is acute and feeling is running high, local vigilante groups will spring into action; but usually a more routine course is followed: long, grim "legal" documents are drawn up covering agreements among wide groups of white home-owners who pledge not to sell their property to us blacks under any circumstances. They call these agreements "restrictive covenants," and in time they grow to be as powerful a detriment to us as had been the policies of the Lords of the Land in the South. In many of the large cities of the United States these agreements affect 80 per cent of all real estate, and they are hailed by the Bosses of the Buildings as the "solution," and the real-estate profits which accrue from our kitchenettes are thereby guaranteed.

Though the United States Supreme Court has so far adroitly avoided rendering a direct decision as to the constitutionality of these restrictive covenants, almost all state, county, and city courts invariably pronounce them "legal." Sometimes ponderous judges point out to us black folk that the real justice of their judgment lies in the fact that we black folk can organize our own property-owning associations and exclude white folk, if we so desire! The courts therefore juggle words so that these restrictive covenants are always "constitutional" and in defense of public policy, thereby assuming the role of policemen in enforcing residential segregation. Newspapers, radios, Protestant and Catholic churches, Jewish synagogues, clubs, civic groups, fraternities, sororities, leagues, and universities bring their moral precepts to bolster their locking-in of hundreds of thousands of us black folk in single, constricted areas. Once again the evils which we thought we had fled forever come back; once again educational appropriations for our black children are curtailed. Local boards of education twist the boundary lines of school districts in such fashion that our boys and girls are legally jim-crowed. The inventive Yankee Bosses of the Buildings go further and contrive even new practices: they reduce the services of the city in our districts; many of our streets remain unlighted at night; violations of fire laws go unpunished; garbage piles up in our alleyways; pavements fall into disrepair; merchants dump tons of their stale and rotten food into the stores and shops of our Black Belts and exact prices as high for these damaged goods as first-rate and grade-A commodities sell for in other sections of the city. Even in times of peace some of the neighborhoods in which we live look as though they had been subjected to an intensive and prolonged aerial bombardment.

Because we are eager to escape these marked-off areas of life, we usually pay more for our homes than whites pay for those of similar value. The Bosses of the Buildings increase their selling prices when they see our black faces. We pay the first installment and then, usually, every member of our family who is able-bodied must work in order to help meet future payments, for our wages are low and our jobs are restricted. Often we move into one room of our new home and rent the remaining rooms to lodgers. Buying homes is a gamble for us black folk in northern cities; completing the purchase depends upon a lot of factors far beyond our control. A depression may throw us out of our low-paying jobs and then we lose our property. Or the health of one or more of the members of our family may fail in the hard grind of a city life that is still new and strange to us.

The Bosses of the Buildings seldom repair the kitchenettes in which we live, and day after day our children romp and play in the hallways and on the stairways until the old buildings sway and creak as though ready to fall in the first high wind. Often the Bosses of the Buildings refuse to pay taxes to the city on Black Belt property, for they know that the amount of accumulated taxes will soon exceed the actual value of the buildings. After they have wrung from us the last bit of profit, they allow the city to assume control of the dilapidated property. And when whole areas of our Black Belt have become filled with condemned buildings which are dangerous for human habitation, the officials of the city will decide that it is unwise to demolish them, for the majority of us black folk would be without shelter, inasmuch as the rest of the city is barred against us.

If you want to see how crowdedly we live, if you want to know how our meager incomes force our families to "double up" to save space, visit a kitchenette building in some Black Belt and look at the long list of American names under our mail boxes: Jackson, Jefferson, Harrison, Grant, Adams, Johnson, Wilson, Madison, Washington, Taylor. . . . So many of us are forced to live in one building that you would think you were reading a crude telephone directory or a clumsy census report when you see our names scrawled on the walls of a thousand dingy vestibules.

Because the Lords of the Land did not build schools for us, many of us know no trades. When applying for a job, we are asked: "What can you do?"

We reply simply and naïvely: "Anything."

What we mean, of course, is that we know nothing but manual labor. Hence, while the Irishman, the Scot, the Croat, the Welshman, the Frenchman, the Spaniard, to whom opportunities are open, merge with the river of American life, we black folk remain out of touch with the quickening fluids of American hope.

In the main, we black folk earn our living in two ways in the northern cities: we work as domestics or as laborers. Our work inside the homes of the Bosses of the Buildings does not differ greatly from the work we did in the homes of the Lords of the Land. But it is in industry that we encounter experiences that tend to break down the structure of our folk characters and project us toward the vortex of modern urban life. It is when we are handling picks rather than mops, it is when we are swinging hammers rather than brooms, it is when we are pushing levers rather than dust-cloths that we are gripped and influenced by the world-wide forces that shape and mold the life of Western civilization. We load and unload the ships and trains, demolish and erect buildings, wheel barrows of cement and sand, pound steel spikes into miles of railroad track, lay brick, drive heavy trucks of lumber and gravel, butcher hogs and sheep and cattle, dig ore, and mine coal.

During the First World War we find plenty of jobs. We are hired at low wages and perform the heavy and dirty work, work which the poor white workers call "nigger work." Our choice is a hard and narrow one, but we make it. Our choice is between eating and starving, and we choose to eat. Mainly our jobs in industry come to us through two routes: (1) strike-breaking and (2) when factories and mills expand so rapidly that not enough white workers can be found to work in them. Here is how it happens: the white workers, the majority of whom will not admit us to membership in their powerful trade unions, go out on strike against the wage cuts and long hours imposed by the Bosses of the Buildings, to whom color is of less significance than profits. To break the strike, the Bosses of the Buildings appeal to us black folk to work; they send labor agents into the South to fetch us north; they promise us "protection"; they tell us that they are our "best friends." We are hungry and eager to work, and yet we know that if we work we will be taking the jobs of other men, and we do not want to do that. We do not want to be scabs; we do not want to be strike-breakers; we do not want to snatch food from the tables of poor white children, for we, of all people, really know how hungry children can be. But, again, we say that we have no choice, and the white workers are emphatic in drawing the color line against us. So, trembling and scared, we take spikes, knives, guns, and break the picket lines and work for the Bosses of the Buildings for our daily bread. And when the work day is over, we find ourselves fighting mobs of white workers in the city streets. After scores of such battles in many cities, after much blood is shed, we black folk gain a precarious foothold in the industries of the North.

But even after we are steadily employed in these industries, the Bosses of the Buildings arrange our lives so that we remain a constant threat to the poor white union workers, who now hate us more than ever for having broken their strike and driven down their wages. But still they refuse to admit us to union membership. Surreptitiously, the Bosses of the Buildings counsel us black folk to have nothing to do with the white workers; they tell us that "good white people" have given us our jobs and we can retain them only if we keep to ourselves. They help us to build churches; they make donations to our institutions; they generally ingratiate themselves as benefactors. And to us, men with simple folk minds, men who have been long used to dealing with other men and not with organizations, this seems sensible and right. So we follow the lead of the Bosses of the Buildings.

The Bosses of the Buildings are much shrewder than the white workers; they place us black folk in the most strategic positions in their plants; they create entire departments for us and place black straw-bosses over us to tell us what to do.

And we feel proud, for we know that the trade unions of the white workers will not sanction such advances as this for us. Yet, deep down, we know the motives that prompt the Bosses of the Buildings to do this for us; in fact, they tell us quite frankly: "Listen, you boys, we are making you boss of this whole department, but we want you to keep away from the white boys, see? We're paying you higher wages than they get, and when they go out on strike we want you boys to carry on."

And we say: "Yes, sir. Thank you, sir."

The white workers, in turn, are wary of us. For generations our labor has been pitted against theirs and their living standards have in many instances been dragged down below even ours. It is an old, sore problem that evokes unreasonable attitudes when it is discussed. Guilty feelings on both sides make it difficult for us to work alongside one another in the mills and factories. We strive for trade-union membership, but the white workers bar us. So we turn to the Bosses of the Buildings, just as in the South we turned to the Lords of the Land, and beg for help. And we get help, but at what a price!

To divide and exploit us still further, the Bosses of the Buildings send their "mouthpieces," their gangster-politicians, to us to preach a gospel that sounds good. They tell us that old Abe Lincoln's party, the Grand Old Party, the Republican Party, is "a ship and all else is the sea"; they explain to us that the Republican Party freed us and is therefore our "natural friend," and that we would be "selling our birthright for a mess of pottage" if we voted for any other party. Our naïve folk minds become lost in the labyrinth of this reasoning. For centuries we have had to rely on the word of others instead of on our own judgment and organized strength; so, with the memory of the Lords of the Land still vivid in our minds, with the image of the hard face of the riding boss still lingering before our eyes, we are swept by our simple fears and hopes into the toils of the gangster-politicians.

Innocently, we vote into office men to whom the welfare of our lives is of far less concern than yesterday's baseball score. The gangster-politicians play a tricky game. In the realm of politics, just as in the realm of jobs, the Bosses of the Buildings pit us against the prejudiced white population and in turn pit them against us. It operates somewhat like this: they make us afraid and then offer to save us. During election campaigns the gangster-politicians come into black neighborhoods and inform us that the whites are planning to attack us, and they tell us that they, and they alone, are our friends and will protect us if we vote for them. Then they go to the be-wildered whites and tell them that we black folk plan to attack them; and then they pose as the friends of the whites and propose to protect *them* against *us*. They ask our black boys to work for them, to become precinct captains, and our boys consent, for here is the promise of a job behind a desk, the kind of job that the white population does not want us to have. In exchange for our vote the gangster-politicians sometimes give us so many petty jobs that the white newspapers in certain northern cities con-temptuously refer to their city hall as "Uncle Tom's Cabin."

Usually our voting strength constitutes the balance of power in those northern cities where the population is divided by the artificially stimulated animosities of many races, and the gangster-politicians, once our vote has established them in the power of office, grant a free hand to the Bosses of the Buildings to proceed with a policy of dishonesty against *all* the citizens of the city.

Yet through the years our loyalty to these gangster-politicians remains stanch because they are almost the only ones who hold out their hands to help us, whatever their motives. They induce enduring sentiments of gratitude among us simple folk. It is the gangster-politician who distributes baskets of food to our poor black families at Christmas time; it is the gangster-politician who advises the distraught black home-owner who is about to become a victim of a mortgage foreclosure; it is the gangster-politician who directs the black plantation-born grandmother to a dentist to have her teeth pulled; it is the gangster-politician who bargains our black boys out of jail when they clash with the law. The Bosses of the Buildings declare that they will not be taxed to build social agencies among us black folk, and the gangster-politicians, passionate seekers of political power, are thereby enabled to perform the function that the social consciousness of the city should perform, granting favors to us in return for votes that place them in political office. The most paradoxical gift ever tendered to us black folk in the city is aid from the underworld, from the gangster, from the political thief. The law says that we are *all* free, but the Bosses of the Buildings say that only *they* are free. We are caught in a tangle of conflicting ideals; we must either swap our votes for bread or starve.

The white workers come to feel that the gangster-politicians are taking their wages from them in the form of high taxes, and they blame us black folk for voting them into power. The white workers charge that we black folk corrupt the life of the city, menace their wages, lengthen their hours of work, decrease the value of their very homes in the neighborhoods where we both live. Of course all this is only relatively true, but the Bosses of the Buildings have so ordered the structure of the lives of both black and white that it is only through a heroic effort of will that either of us can cast off this spell of make-believe and see how artificial and man-made is this enmity between us, to see that our common lives are bound by a common cause.

The majority of both black and white, however, live under the spell wrought by the Bosses of the Buildings. During the years following the First World War a depression grips the nation and the poor white workers, frantic and embittered, begin to push us out of our jobs. We can be waiters no longer, for the Bosses of the Buildings, to appease the unrest of the white workers, grant them the honor of serving tables in many hotels and cafés. They feel that it is wiser to give them our jobs than to let them go idle and think and organize. In many cities, where there was a black porter there is now a white porter. In many apartments white cooks replace black cooks. As our unemployment increases, the Bosses of the Buildings pay more taxes to feed us and we sit in our kitchenettes and wonder.

Bloody riots break forth over trifling incidents that would ordinarily be forgotten in the routine of daily living. Throughout the North tension mounts. The atmosphere grows ripe for violence. We feel it coming. Still we go to the scab jobs for bread. Then, suddenly, over anything, over an imagined insult, over an altercation between a black boy and a white boy on a beach, over the wild rumor that a white man has slapped a black boy in a store, over the whispered tale that some white man has spoken improperly to a black girl, over the fact that a black man has accidentally stepped on a white woman's foot, over the gossip that a black woman has talked back to a white woman—it matters not what the pretext is!—street-fighting, protracted, bitter, sanguine, flares in Pittsburgh, Chicago, Washington, New York, Atlanta, and East St. Louis. They kill us and we kill them. We both feel that we are right. This is what life comes to when men's minds are snared in darkness and confusion. . . .

State troops come and impose order. When the fighting is over, we bind up our wounds and count our dead, and another day finds us still marching forward for jobs. Again we say, of the North as of the South, that life for us is daily warfare and that we live hard, like soldiers. We are set apart from the civilian population; our kitchenettes comprise our barracks; the color of our skins constitutes our uniforms; the streets of our cities are our trenches; a job is a pill-box to be captured and held; and the unions of white workers for a long time have formed the first line of resistance which we encounter. The gangster-politicians are our captains, the men who lead us into the immediate assault. The Bosses of the Buildings are the generals who decree the advance or retreat. We are always in battle, but the tidings of victory are few.

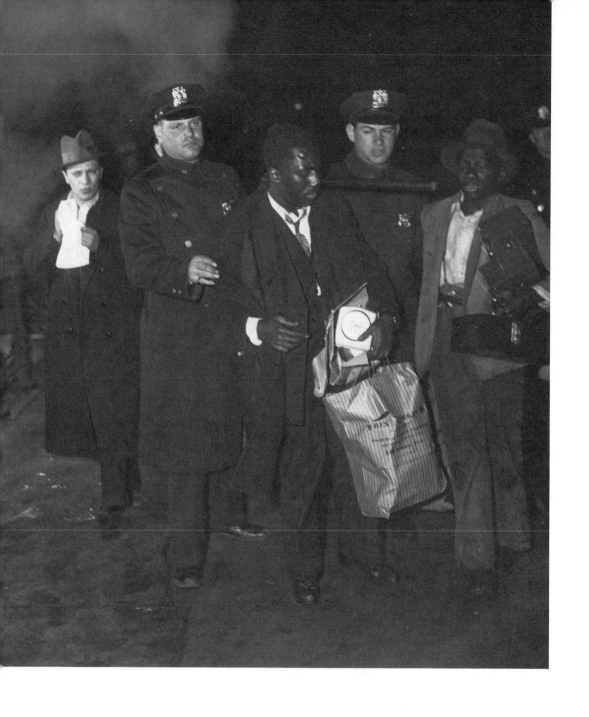

We are always in battle

The tidings of victory are few

When off duty after a hard day of fighting, we are like spent troops, ready to plunge into pleasure to obliterate the memory of this slow death on the city pavements. Just as in the South, in spite of the Lords of the Land, we managed to keep alive deep down in us a hope of what life could be, so now, with death ever hard at our heels, we pour forth in song and dance, without stint or shame, a sense of what our bodies want, a hint of our hope of a full life lived without fear, a whisper of the natural dignity we feel life can have, a cry of hunger for something new to fill our souls, to reconcile the ecstasy of living with the terror of dying. . . .

It is when we seek to express ourselves that the paradoxical cleavage in our lives shows most. Day after day we labor in the gigantic factories and mills of Western civilization, but we have never been allowed to become an organic part of this civilization; we have yet to share its ultimate hopes and expectations. Its incentives and perspectives, which form the core of meaning for so many millions, have yet to lift our personalities to levels of purpose. Instead, after working all day in one civilization, we go home to our Black Belts and live, within the orbit of the surviving remnants of the culture of the South, our naïve, casual, verbal, fluid folk life.

Alone together with our black folk in the towering tenements, we play our guitars, trumpets, and pianos, beating out rough and infectious rhythms that create an instant appeal among all classes of people. Why is our music so contagious? Why is it that those who deny us are willing to sing our songs? Perhaps it is because so many of those who live in cities feel deep down just as we feel. Our big brass horns, our huge noisy drums and whirring violins make a flood of melodies whose poignancy is heightened by our latent fear and uneasiness, by our love of the sensual, and by our feverish hunger for life. On the plantations our songs carried a strain of other-worldly yearning which people called "spiritual"; but now our blues, jazz, swing, and boogie-woogie are our "spirituals" of the city pavements, our longing for freedom and opportunity, an expression of our bewilderment and despair in a world whose meaning eludes us. The ridiculousness and sublimity of love are captured in our blues, those sad-happy songs that laugh and weep all in one breath, those mockingly tender utterances of a folk imprisoned in steel and stone. Our thirst for the sensual is poured out in jazz; the tension of our brittle lives is given forth in swing; and our nervousness and exhaustion are pounded out in the swift tempo of boogie-woogie.

We lose ourselves in violent forms of dances in our ballrooms. The faces of the white world, looking on in wonder and curiosity, declare: *"Only the Negro can play!"* But they are wrong. They misread us. We are able to play in this fashion because we have been excluded, left behind; we play in this manner because all excluded folk play. The English say of the Irish, just as America says of us, that only the Irish can play, that they laugh through their tears. But every powerful nation says this of the folk whom it oppresses in justification of that oppression. And, ironically, they are angered by the exhibition of any evidence to the contrary, for it disturbs their conscience with vague and guilty doubts. They smile with cold disdain when we black folk say that our thirst can be slaked in art, that our tensions can be translated into industry, that our energies can be applied to finance, that our delight in the world can be converted into education, that our love of adventure can find fulfillment in aviation. But in one way or another, the white folk deny us these pursuits, and our hunger for expression finds its form in our wild, raw music, in our invention of slang that winds its way all over America. Our adoration of color goes not into murals, but into dress, into green, red, yellow, and blue clothes. When we have some money in our pockets on payday, our laughter and songs make the principal streets of our Black Belts—Lenox Avenue, Beale Street, State Street, South Street, Second Street, Auburn Avenue—famous the earth over.

The Bosses of the Buildings would have the world believe that we black folk, after these three hundred years, have locked in our veins blood of a queer kind that makes us act in this "special pattern." In their classrooms and laboratories they attempt to harness science in defense of their attitudes and practices, and never do they so vigorously assail us as "trouble-makers" as when we say that we are "this way" because we are made to live "this way." They say we speak treasonably when we declare that human life is plastic, that human nature is malleable, that men possess the dignity and meaning of the environmental and institutional forms through which they are lucky or unlucky enough to express themselves. They solemnly assert that we seek to overthrow the government by violence when we say that we live in this manner because the Black Belt which cradles our lives is created by the hands and brains of men who have decreed that we must live differently. They brand us as revolutionists when we say that we are not allowed to react to life with an honest and frontal vision.

We live on, and our music makes the feet of the whole world dance, even the feet of the children of the poor white workers who live beyond the line that marks the boundary of our lives. Where we cannot go, our tunes, songs, slang, and jokes go. Some of the white boys and girls, starved prisoners of urban homes, even forget the hatred of their parents when they hear our sensual, wailing blue melodies. The common people of the nation grow to love our songs so much that a few of us make our living by creating a haven of song for those who are weary of the barren world of steel and stone reared by the Bosses of the Buildings. But only a few of those who dance and sing with us suspect the rawness of life out of which our laughing-crying tunes and quick dance-steps come; they do not know that our songs and dances are our banner of hope flung desperately up in the face of a world that has pushed us to the wall.

Despite our new worldliness, despite our rhythms, our colorful speech, and our songs, we keep our churches alive. In fact, we have built more of them than ever here on the city pavements, for it is only when we are within the walls of our churches that we are wholly ourselves, that we keep alive a sense of our personalities in relation to the total world in which we live, that we maintain a quiet and constant communion with all that is deepest in us. Our going to church of a Sunday is like placing one's ear to another's chest to hear the unquenchable murmur of the human heart. In our collective outpourings of song and prayer, the fluid emotions of others make us feel the strength in ourselves. We build great churches, some of the greatest in terms of membership—some of our churches have more than 20,000 members—ever built in the history of Western civilization. Our churches are where we dip our tired bodies in cool springs of hope, where we retain our wholeness and humanity despite the blows of death from the Bosses of the Buildings.

Our churches are centers of social and community life, for we have virtually no other mode of communion and we are usually forbidden to worship God in the temples of the the Bosses of the Buildings. The church is the door through which we first walked into Western civilization; religion is the form in which America first allowed our personalities to be expressed. Our churches provide social activities for us, cook and serve meals, organize baseball and basketball teams, operate stores and businesses, and conduct social agencies. Our first newspapers and magazines are launched from our churches.

In the Black Belts of the northern cities, our women are the most circumscribed and tragic objects to be found in our lives, and it is to the churches that our black women cling for emotional security and the release of their personalities. Because their orbit of life is narrow—from their kitchenette to the white folk's kitchen and back home again—they love the church more than do our men, who find a large measure of the expression of their lives in the mills and factories. Surrounding our black women are many almost insuperable barriers: they are black, they are women, they are workers; they are triply anchored and restricted in their movements within and without the Black Belts.

From the kitchenette . . .

. . . to the white folk's kitchen

So they keep thousands of Little Bethels and Pilgrims and Calvarys and White Rocks and Good Hopes and Mount Olives going with their nickels and dimes. Nurtured in the close and intimate folk culture of the South, where each person knew the others, where the basic emotions of life were shared by all, many of them sometimes feel that the elaborate ritual of our big churches is too cold and formal for them. To retain the ardent religious emotionalism of which they are so fond, many of them will group themselves about a lonely young black preacher and help him to establish what is called a "store front" church, in which they are still able to perform their religious rituals on the fervid levels of the plantation revival. Sometimes, even in crowded northern cities, elderly black women, hungry for the South but afraid to return, will cultivate tiny vegetable gardens in the narrow squares of ground in front of their hovels. More than even that of the American Indian, the consciousness of vast sections of our black women lies beyond the boundaries of the modern world, though they live and work in that world daily.

Outside of the church, many of our black women drift to ruin and death on the pavements of the city; they are sold, by white men as well as by black, for sex purposes. As a whole, they must go to work at an earlier age than any other section of the nation's population. For every 5 white girls between the ages of ten and fifteen who must work, 25 of our black girls must work; for every 5 white mothers who must leave their children unattended at home in order to work, 25 of our black mothers must leave their children unattended at home in order to work. As modernity and complexity spread through the cities, our black women find that their jobs grow fewer. Many white folk send their soiled clothes to the laundry and hire Japanese, Chinese, and Filipinos as servants to do their domestic work.

Many of our children scorn us; they say that we still wear the red bandanna about our heads, that we are still Uncle Toms. We lean upon our God and scold our children and try to drag them to church with us, but just as we once, years ago, left the plantation to roam the South, so now they leave us for the city pavements. But deep down in us we are glad that our children feel the world hard enough to yearn to wrestle with it. We, the mothers and fathers of the black children, try to hold them back from death, but if we persuade them to stay, or if they come back because we call them, we will pour out our pity upon them. Always our deepest love is toward those children of ours who turn their backs upon our way of life, for our instincts tell us that those brave ones who struggle against death are the ones who bring new life into the world, even though they die to do so, even though our hearts are broken when they die.

We watch strange moods fill our children, and our hearts swell with pain. The streets, with their noise and flaring lights, the taverns, the automobiles, and the poolrooms claim them, and no voice of ours can call them back. They spend their nights away from home; they forget our ways of life, our language, our God. Their swift speech and impatient eyes make us feel weak and foolish. We cannot keep them in school; more than 1,000,000 of our black boys and girls of high school age are not in school. We fall upon our knees and pray for them, but in vain. The city has beaten us, evaded us; but they, with young bodies filled with warm blood, feel bitter and frustrated at the sight of the alluring hopes and prizes denied them. It is not their eagerness to fight that makes us afraid, but that they go to death on the city pavements faster than even disease and starvation can take them. As the courts and the morgues become crowded with our lost children, the hearts of the officials of the city grow cold toward us. As our jobs begin to fail in another depression, our lives and the lives of our children grow so frightful that even some of our educated black leaders are afraid to make known to the nation how we exist. They became ashamed of us and tell us to hide our wounds. And many white people who know how we live are afraid of us, fearing that we may rise up against them.

The sands of our simple folk lives run out on the cold city pavements. Winter winds blow, and we feel that our time is nearing its end. Our final days are full of apprehension, for our children grapple with the city. We cannot bear to look at them; they struggle against great odds. Our tired eyes turn away as we hear the tumult of battle. . . .

Strange moods fill our children

The streets claim our children

4.

Men in the Making

WE ARE THE CHILDREN of the black sharecroppers, the first-born of the city tenements.

We have tramped down a road three hundred years long. We have been shunted to and fro by cataclysmic social changes.

We are a folk born of cultural devastation, slavery, physical suffering, unrequited longing, abrupt emancipation, migration, disillusionment, bewilderment, joblessness, and insecurity—all enacted within a *short* space of historical time!

There are millions of us and we are moving in all directions. All our lives we have been catapulted into arenas where, had we thought consciously of invading them, we would have hung back. A sense of constant change has stolen silently into our lives and has become operative in our personalities as a law of living.

There are some of us who feel our hurts so deeply that we find it impossible to work with whites; we feel that it is futile to hope or dream in terms of American life. Our distrust is so great that we form intensely racial and nationalistic organizations and advocate the establishment of a separate state, a forty-ninth state, in which we black folk would live.

There are even today among us groups that forlornly plan a return to Africa.

There are others of us who feel the need of the protection of a strong nation so keenly that we admire the harsh and imperialistic policies of Japan and ardently hope that the Japanese will assume the leadership of the "darker races."

As our consciousness changes, as we come of age, as we shed our folk swaddling-clothes, so run our lives in a hundred directions.

Today, all of us black folk are not poor. A few of us have money. We make it as the white folk make theirs, but our money-making is restricted to our own people. Many of us black folk have managed to send our children to school, and a few of our children are now professional and business men whose standards of living approximate those of middle-class whites. Some of us own small businesses; others devote their lives to law and medicine.

But the majority of us still toil on the plantations, work in heavy industry, and labor in the kitchens of the Lords of the Land and the Bosses of the the Buildings.

The general dislocation of life during the depression caused many white workers to learn through chronic privation that they could not protect their standards of living so long as we blacks were excluded from their unions.

Many hundreds of thousands of them found that they could not fight successfully for increased wages and union recognition unless we stood shoulder to shoulder with them. As a consequence, many of us have recently become members of steel, auto, packing, and tobacco unions.

In 1929, when millions of us black folk were jobless, many unemployed white workers joined with us on a national scale to urge relief measures and adequate housing. The influence of this united effort spread even into the South where black and white sharecroppers were caught in the throes of futile conflict.

The fears of black and white lessened in the face of the slowly widening acceptance of an identity of interests. When the depression was at its severest, the courts of many cities, at the instigation of the Bosses of the Buildings, sent armed marshals to evict our jobless black families for their inability to pay rent for the rotting kitchenettes. Organized into groups, we black folk smashed the marshals' locks, picked up the paltry sticks of furniture, and replaced the evicted families. Having hurdled fear's first barrier, we found that many white workers were eager to have us in their organizations, and we were proud to feel that at last our strength was sufficient to awaken in others a desire to work with us. These men differed from those whom we had known on the plantations; they were not "po' white trash." We invited them into our homes and broke our scanty bread with them, and this was our supreme gesture of trust. In this way we encountered for the first time in our lives the full effect of those forces that tended to reshape our folk consciousness, and a few of us stepped forth and accepted within the confines of our personalities the death of our old folk lives, an acceptance of a death that enabled us to cross class and racial lines, a death that made us free.

Not all black folk, however, reacted to the depression in this manner. There were hundreds of thousands of us who saw that we bought our groceries from white clerks, that we paid our insurance to white agents, that we paid our rent to white realtors, that our children were taught in school by white teachers, that we were served in hospitals by white doctors, that we asked jobs of white bosses, that we paid our fares on busses and street cars to white conductors; in short, that we had no word to say about anything that happened in our lives. In 1935, inarticulate black men and women, filled with a naive, peasant anger, rioted in Harlem's business district and wrought a property damage of more than $2,000,000!

But our most qualitatively significant progress was organized and conducted through peaceful channels. In many large cities there were sturdy minorities of us, both black and white, who banded together in disciplined, class-conscious groups and created new organs of action and expression. We were able to seize nine black boys in a jail in Scottsboro, Alabama, lift them so high in our collective hands, focus such a battery of comment and interpretation upon them, that they became symbols to all the world of the plight of black folk in America.

If we had been allowed to participate in the vital processes of America's national growth, what would have been the texture of our lives, the pattern of our traditions, the routine of our customs, the state of our arts, the code of our laws, the function of our government! Whatever others may say, we black folk say that America would have been stronger and greater!

Standing now at the apex of the twentieth century, we look back over the road we have traveled and compare it with the road over which the white folk have traveled, and we see that three hundred years in the history of our lives are equivalent to two thousand years in the history of the lives of whites! The many historical phases which whites have traversed voluntarily and gradually during the course of Western civilization we black folk have traversed through swift compulsion. During the three hundred years we have been in the New World, we have experienced all the various types of family life, all the many adjustments to rural and urban life, and today, weary but still eager, we stand ready to accept more change.

Imagine European history from the days of Christ to the present telescoped into three hundred years and you can comprehend the drama which our consciousness has experienced! Brutal, bloody, crowded with suffering and abrupt transitions, the lives of us black folk represent the most magical and meaningful picture of human experience in the Western world. Hurled from our native African homes into the very center of the most complex and highly industrialized civilization the world has ever known, we stand today with a consciousness and memory such as few people possess.

We black folk, our history and our present being, are a mirror of all the manifold experiences of America. What we want, what we represent, what we endure is what America *is*. If we black folk perish, America will perish. If America has forgotten her past, then let her look into the mirror of our consciousness and she will see the *living* past living in the present, for our memories go back, through our black folk of today, through the recollections of our black parents, and through the tales of slavery told by our black grandparents, to the time when none of us, black or white, lived in this fertile land.

The differences between black folk and white folk are not blood or color, and the ties that bind us are deeper than those that separate us. The common road of hope which we all have traveled has brought us into a stronger kinship than any words, laws, or legal claims.

Look at us and know us and you will know yourselves, for *we* are *you*, looking back at you from the dark mirror of our lives!

What do we black folk want?

We want what others have, the right to share in the upward march of American life, the only life we remember or have ever known.

The Lords of the Land say: "We will not grant this!"

We answer: "We ask you to grant us nothing. We are winning our heritage, though our toll in suffering is great!"

The Bosses of the Buildings say: "Your problem is beyond solution!"

We answer: "Our problem is being solved. We are crossing the line you dared us to cross, though we pay in the coin of death!"

The seasons of the plantation no longer dictate the lives of many of us; hundreds of thousands of us are moving into the sphere of conscious history.

We are with the new tide. We stand at the crossroads. We watch each new procession. The hot wires carry urgent appeals. Print compels us. Voices are speaking. Men are moving! And we shall be with them. . . .

About the Photographs

THE PHOTOGRAPHS in this book—with the exception of a few otherwise credited—were selected from the files of the Farm Security Administration, U.S. Department of Agriculture. They form part of a document on contemporary America which at this writing has reached a total of some 65,000 pictures. None of the photographs here reproduced was made for this book; they were taken by Farm Security photographers as they roamed the country during a five-year period on their regular assignments.

I wish to thank Mr. Roy E. Stryker, chief of the Historical Section, Farm Security Administration, for his never-failing interest, courtesy, and co-operation; and Mr. Horace R. Cayton, director of the Good Shepherd Community Center, Chicago, Illinois, for his invaluable advice on the pictorial interpretation of the urban Negro.

EDWIN ROSSKAM

THE PICTURES

Jacket. *Russell Lee:* Church service, Illinois. FSA*

Title Page. *Edwin Rosskam:* Street scene, Chicago, Ill. FSA

PAGE

9. *Dorothea Lange:* Sharecropper's hands, Alabama. FSA

10. *Jack Delano:* Sharecropper, Georgia. FSA

11. *Russell Lee:* Trash collector, Chicago, Ill. FSA

18. *Jack Delano:* Maid, Washington, D.C. FSA

19. *Arthur Rothstein:* Steelworker, Pennsylvania. FSA

20. *Russell Lee:* Stevedores, Houston, Tex. FSA

*From Farm Security Administration

*From U.S. Office of War Information

E 185.6 W9 1988
OCLC 16868125
12 million black voices /
Wright, Richard.

DATE DUE

NOV 11 2013

GAYLORD   PRINTED IN U.S.A.